PRAYING *for* RAIN

PRAYING *for* RAIN

NANCIE CARMICHAEL

SURRENDER & TRIUMPH IN LIFE'S
DESERT EXPERIENCES

THOMAS NELSON PUBLISHERS
Nashville

Published in Nashville, Tennessee, by Thomas Nelson, Inc.

Unless otherwise noted, Scripture quotations are from THE NEW KING JAMES VERSION of the Bible. Copyright © 1979, 1980, 1982, 1990, 1994, Thomas Nelson, Inc., Publishers.

Scripture quotations noted AMPLIFIED BIBLE are from THE AMPLIFIED BIBLE: Old Testament. Copyright © 1962, 1964 by Zondervan Publishing House (used by permission); and from THE AMPLIFIED NEW TESTAMENT. Copyright © 1958 by the Lockman Foundation (used by permission).

Scripture quotations noted KJV are from The Holy Bible, KING JAMES VERSION.

Scripture quotations noted TLB are from THE LIVING BIBLE (Wheaton, Illinois: Tyndale House Publishers, 1971) and are used by permission.

Scripture quotations noted NIV are taken from the HOLY BIBLE, NEW INTERNATIONAL VERSION®. Copyright © 1973, 1978, 1984 by International Bible Society. Used by permission of Zondervan Bible Publishing House. All rights reserved.

The "NIV" and "New International Version" trademarks are registered in the United States Patent and Trademark Office by International Bible Society. Use of either trademark requires the permission of International Bible Society.

Scripture quotations noted NLT are from THE HOLY BIBLE, NEW LIVING TRANSLATION, copyright © 1996. Used by permission of Tyndale House Publishers, Inc., Wheaton, IL 60189. All rights reserved.

ISBN 0-7852-6782-4

Printed in the United States of America
1 2 3 4 5 6 7 PHX 05 04 03 02 01

CONTENTS

~

INTRODUCTION:
WHY WRITE ABOUT THIS?

> O God, you are my God
>> I earnestly search for you.
> My soul thirsts for you;
>> my whole body longs for you
>> in this parched and weary land
>> where there is no water.
>>> —Psalm 63:1, NLT

When I tell people I'm writing about the desert, usually there's an immediate recognition, often a wry smile: "Can we talk?" Although we all may describe the desert experience in different ways—and it comes in different forms—we know it when we're there. It is part of being human. And if we live long enough, we experience the desert just as sure as part of earth's physical landscape is desert.

What is a desert experience, anyway? It may help to

describe the desert by saying what it is *not*. It isn't a problem or a sticky situation. It may start out that way, but the desert is actually a *place*. You become engulfed by a need, a loss, or a circumstance. You feel surrounded. You can no longer cope; it's no longer business as usual. It may be caused by many things: a major illness, a divorce, a job loss. It may be a depression. It may be caused by the loss of a family member or close friend. It may be a stressful marriage, or the sense of being stuck in a negative situation. It may be the result of burnout, of exhaustion; of working hard on a project only to have it fail.

It could be a sense of isolation after moving somewhere and your friends and family are far away. Or it may be you just wandered into the desert through lack of direction or through no fault of your own. Your desert experience may be unexplainable, just an overwhelming sense that nothing right is happening and your expectations and dreams are frustrated, delayed. Maybe you don't know why; *you only know that life is hard*.

Some of us live "closer" to the desert experience than others, maybe because of circumstances or simply because of our outlook and temperament. In writing this, I'm reminded that I do live close to the desert, figuratively as well as literally. (Yes, I tend to see the glass as "half-empty"!)

BENEFITS OF THE DESERT EXPERIENCE

Our mountain family home is surrounded by stately ponderosa pine trees nestled close to the beautiful snow-covered

Cascade range. The area where we live is green and lush with vegetation, wildlife, streams, and lakes. Yet only thirty miles east of here is a desert that stretches over several hundred miles. Many who hear of the famous green and rain of Oregon don't realize the state is at least one-third desert. So while I live in a forested place, I also live close to the desert. I drive through it often on my way to places I need to go. And while I have a natural aversion to the desert and would not deliberately go there, the longer I live, the more I am drawn to its austere beauty. The more I study it and stay with it, the more I realize the benefits it offers.

So, too, with the spiritual deserts of my life. While I would not choose to go there, I am realizing the enormous gifts that the desert offers to my sometimes hectic and overcommitted life. Without periodic visits to the desert, I would not listen to God half so intently. It also is an opportunity to get away from the distracting noise of life, an opportunity to see the big picture.

A PART OF LIFE'S JOURNEY

Pretty daunting, the desert. Who would choose to deliberately go there? The children of Israel had to go through a desert wilderness to reach the promised land. And in our country's own history, several hundred thousand pioneers had to cross sections of desert to reach their own "promised land" in their quest for something better. It was an enormous personal sacrifice for them to leave their homes and parents, not to mention the dangerous and difficult journey. And yet they kept going, knowing they had to go through it to get to the fertile land. Crossing the desert was simply part of the journey.

And so it is with our lives. It's part of our experience—and an instructive one at that. The desert wilderness can refine us, reveal who we are, and help to clarify our purpose. Jesus prepared for His earthly ministry forty days and nights in a desert place. John the Baptist preached from a desert wilderness. Moses heard God from a burning bush in the back side of the desert.

Today we are blessed with many options and choices with which to fill our lives, and while that is good, it can also add to our sense of being overwhelmed. It seems we never have enough time—time just to process life; therefore, many people today live in a quiet state of despair and pressure. What has changed radically for us from our parents' generation is not that we are working so much harder, but that our sense of *what is necessary* in our lives has increased. We cram our days, weeks, and expectations full.

I learned this professionally as well as personally. With my fifteen-plus years of experience in publishing and editing women's magazines, I have been privileged to read many demographic surveys and letters from women. In one survey of *Virtue* magazine readers, we asked about their lives. Nearly three thousand responses came back from women. Although they led varied lives, one theme was overwhelmingly consistent, and one woman seemed to speak for most: "I have too much to do; too little time to do it in. I am up to here physically, financially, spiritually, emotionally. I can't handle one more thing." This sense of "too much" seemed to affect her overall life. She was barely coping, treading water and somewhat bewildered at how hard life was. Women do have unique pressures today—they face not only the pressure of caring for family but also of working, earning money. Christian women have the additional pressure of keeping their children from negative cultural influences and the pressure to make a difference. Men, too, are in the pressure cooker of life as they face challenges that are unique to them in providing financially and every other way for themselves and their families.

Desert experiences happen for many reasons, not just an overload of stress. We all suffer losses and disappointments and frustrating times of waiting. Not long ago, I did a survey among several hundred individuals, asking them to describe a time when God met them. It was insightful to see that it was in their most difficult, desperate time when they sensed God's intervention in their lives.[1]

These were not just facts or surveys to me; I identified all too painfully with them. I have been a Christian for many years, and yet I went through a time in my late thirties when I no longer wanted to live. I was in a serious depression from some accumulated losses and also from the fact that I was running in the red emotionally, physically, and spiritually. But as I finally had the courage to open my eyes to the truth of my life, I began to hear God as never before, and I saw that because of my unwelcomed desert experiences, my life has become richer, more honest, and more productive. Before my own desert experience, I never seemed to have enough time to process life.

The desert intruded, offering me a place to make time for things that really matter.

Each of us is living a beautiful, complicated, and challenging life. Each of us will have our share of life's hardships and sorrows. I have noticed that two different people can have the same adversity; one will triumph while the other will be defeated. What makes the difference? I believe our response in the desert place is the key. The paradox of the desert is that if you cultivate it, it can become a beautiful, productive garden. Or it can draw the very life out of you and you end up just existing.

TRUST GOD AND HIS WORD

Popular thought encourages us to "listen to our inner voice"; therein lie empowerment and wisdom. This is a subtle twist of the truth. Of course it's important to pay attention to our feelings, to realize what's going on inside. Christians have notoriously denied feelings, denied pain. But the key to success in the wilderness is to know God's Word in the midst of our pain and confusion and to trust Him, obey Him. If we do not, there is nothing to keep us from despair and confusion. The children of Israel left Egypt to go to the promised land, and what should have been an eleven-day journey turned into a forty-year saga of misery. Why? Because they resisted God's voice in the wilderness. They were consumed by their own hungers and complaints. Listening to our own complaints in the desert is not enough. When we can listen to

God's voice through His life-giving Word, He will rebuild our brokenness.

With each chapter in this book, I have made a point to use a scriptural illustration with the concept, along with suggested reading, because, ultimately, that is what will feed you and help to restore your life. Human wisdom or experience is not enough. You must have the life-giving, life-nourishing, life-changing Word of God, which will, through the Holy Spirit, show you what you need for the rest of your journey.

As you go through this book, perhaps one chapter will speak to you more than another. I deliberately tried to write each chapter so that it could stand on its own if necessary. When I was in my own desert experience, I wasn't up to reading a full-blown treatise on the desert experience. I needed to have something targeted to where I was, something I could pick up and put down. Prayerfully consider what is going on in your life, and how you can respond to God in it. Take time to journal, to reflect. Take God's Word into your own experience and learn from it, respond to it. Remember that the desert experience often comes before a period of great creativity and usefulness and it can energize your life, instruct you, and prepare you for the next step.

Although this book was surprisingly difficult to write because it took me back so vividly to the hardest times of my life, it also helped me appreciate again God's infinite plan in all of life, not just the green pastures. I am reminded of how profound the lessons are if we will only listen. It is my passion in this book to encourage you to honestly look at your life;

indeed, to embrace your desert experience and allow it to become a place of letting go and of surrender to God. It can be a pivotal place of opportunity to learn as never before about God and lead you to a wonderful place of triumph and purpose.

I go forward, but He is not there,
And backward, but I cannot perceive Him;
When He works on the left hand, I cannot behold Him;
When He turns to the right hand, I cannot see Him.
But He knows the way that I take;
When He has tested me, I shall come forth as gold.

—JOB 23:8–10

1

~

WHAT AM I DOING HERE?

The word of the LORD came to him, and He said to
him, "What are you doing here, Elijah?"

—1 Kings 19:9

— SUGGESTED READING: 1 KINGS 17; 18; 19 —

A WAKE-UP CALL

I was lying in a doctor's office, staring at the beige wall
while I waited for the results of a spinal tap. I'd had to
lie flat for some time after the test, and the last thing the
doctor said to me before leaving was a worried, "If this
lupus is affecting your central nervous system, it could be
fatal." And that's when I asked myself, *What am I doing here?*
I don't have time for this. I have a busy husband, five children . . .
places to go, people to see.

It had started several years previously. About that time, I'd written in my journal:

> *Had blood and urinalysis at the lab this morning. I will go back later to see if there's some physical reason for the way I feel: fatigue, depression, constant headache, aching joints, swollen lymph glands. I can't think clearly, which bothers me a lot. I'm not doing anything well. What is wrong with me? Every day I search for a Scripture that will help me get through the day: "God will supply my every need" or, "I can do all things through Christ." But there are some days I cannot even grasp hold of a Scripture or thought and I feel as though I'm at the bottom of a well, screaming "Help!" to the top.*

At first, after many trips to various doctors, there seemed to be no diagnosis, and the aching in my joints, fatigue, and depression hung on. The doctor prescribed medication for pain and antidepressants for depression. The side effects of the drugs at times were troublesome, and I would try something else. Finally, after more tests that showed a positive ANA blood test (indicating the possibility of an autoimmune disease), my doctor told me he thought I had systemic lupus erythematosus.

Having a diagnosis—even though I was dismayed at having lupus—was a relief. At least I had a label, a handle on what was wrong so that I could deal with it and try to get well. I was told the condition was chronic, and the idea of a "chronic" condition was distressing. I wanted to get over it, get rid of it. I had watched my mother live with chronic leukemia, and although she was heroic, I didn't care to be heroic. I prayed, *Great Physician, I need You. I promise, I will learn the deep lessons that are necessary, but then let me get on with life.*

But my health did not get better, and in spite of trying different medications, I seemed to be worse. My face was going numb, and that was why I was at the neurologist's having a spinal tap. With the doctor's words ringing in my ears after he left the room, I remember staring at the wall, feeling absolutely at the bottom. *Lord*, I prayed, *why is this happening to me? What am I doing here, anyway?* It seemed that I heard His still, small voice: *Just let go.* I wondered, *Let go of what?* I only knew how to grab on, to add to my life. I didn't know how to let go, but something was wrong. It was becoming obvious that I was getting a wake-up call for some reason.

All of us are confronted at times with "wake-up calls" in life. We can ignore them, rationalize them away, or we can realize there's something in our lives that needs attention. God does speak to us, if we'll listen. In that moment of confusion and fear, I was forced to pay attention.

"JUST STRESS"

Shortly after this, at my husband's urging, I went to the Mayo Clinic for a thorough examination to see if I could get some concrete answers. After three days of tests, I sat in Dr. O'Duffy's office as he told me, "I find no lupus — congratulations. You are organically and neurologically healthy. I believe that stress is the cause of your pain."

3

I was astounded. "You mean it's just stress?"

"There's no such thing as 'just stress.' Stress causes, or exacerbates, most major illnesses. Your mind, body, and soul are connected. You're a package deal." He looked at my chart, describing my life. "You say you're married to a busy man. You've got five children. You're helping to edit a magazine, run a prison ministry, work in your church. You're on the school board." He asked me frankly, "What is wrong with you? Why do you have to do so much? Who do you think you are—superwoman?" He went on, "If you want, you can have a label—fibromyalgia—and you can continue to take all these medications. Or you can do something that is harder, but in the long run, better. You can go home and confront your life to see why you have so much stress."

I knew I'd been presented with a clear choice. On the plane trip home I felt broken and humbled, and I determined to take the harder but better way. I wasn't used to taking care of myself; I had everybody else to care for. But now I realized that I had a problem only I could address. How had I gotten to that place? And what was I doing there?

OVERWHELMED

Therefore my spirit is overwhelmed within me;
My heart within me is distressed.

—PSALM 143:4

We all have times when life is overwhelming. What do we do then? Often we escape into other things, which doesn't solve our real problem; it only postpones or complicates it. And although none of us want desert experiences, we need them to process life, to hear what God is saying. The desert is actually a gift to us. It is important to recognize we are there, and respond to God's question: What are you doing here? If you have picked up this book, chances are, you recognize that you have been in a desert experience or are in one now. But the key issue is, How will you respond?

A few months after I came back from the Mayo Clinic, while my husband and sons went on a fishing trip, I drove my mother and my daughter back to Montana to visit the family farm. It was a difficult trip. On the way, it became apparent that my mother's Alzheimer's was beginning to seriously affect her. I was also beginning to realize my daughter had more complicated learning disabilities than I'd first thought. At the same time, we were selling our magazine company and trying to let go of some of the reins. Two of our sons were leaving for college that fall. And besides, I was sick. I hurt. I was feeling absolutely overwhelmed, and along the way home to Montana, God and I had a one-sided dialogue with me asking, "Why, God? What's going on? Stress? Who doesn't have stress?" And God wasn't saying anything. It was a bittersweet journey, and as I wondered and prayed, I drank in the beauty of the mountains and the rolling plains of home as we drove.

We stopped for the night at an inn on Lake MacDonald,

where Bill and I had spent our honeymoon years before. The stunning magnificence of the rugged mountains that surrounded the lake was somehow comforting, and their familiar outline against the Montana sky reminded me of the many times I'd been there as a child with my parents and family; then later with my husband. Now to be there when it seemed that everything in my life was eroding reminded me of the timeless promises of God, of eternity. That somehow I'd get through this overwhelming time of life.

That night after I got Mother and Amy safely settled inside our cabin, I put on a jacket and walked along the shore of the lake at dusk, quoting Psalm 91: "He who dwells in the secret place of the Most High shall abide under the shadow of the Almighty. " We drove toward home the next day, and for weeks after that, I found myself quoting Psalm 91 again and again and carrying an image of the mountains and the still waters in my mind: "He shall call upon Me, and I will answer him; I will be with him in trouble; I will deliver him" (v. 15). There was something there for me, although I didn't know what. Perhaps it was the presence of God in the midst of my desert. All I knew was that my back was against the wall, and I was ready to listen to God.

O God my Father, I have no words, no words by which I dare express the things that stir within me. I lay bare myself, my world, before you in the quietness. Brood over my spirit with your great tenderness and understanding and judgment, so that I will find, in some strange new way, strength for my weakness, health for my illness, guidance for my journey. This is the stirring of my heart, O God, my Father. Amen.

—HOWARD THURMAN, *The Growing Edge*[1]

WHAT WE CAN LEARN FROM ELIJAH

The story of the prophet Elijah, whom God used to try to get Israel to listen and return to Him, is a fascinating one and spoke deeply to me about what it means to hear God's voice in the wilderness. It's the story of a nation in a desert experience; and then of the prophet himself ending up in his own desert experience. Drought had been in the land of Israel for three years, a direct result of the people's disobedience and worship of the Baals. In fact it was Elijah who had pronounced the drought in the first place. In 1 Kings 17, we see that there were many who suffered from the drought even though they themselves may not have been involved in the idol worship. The sin of some affected the whole nation.

ELIJAH WAS ZEALOUS FOR GOD'S WORK

In 1 Kings 17, Elijah—who was hungry—encountered a widow picking up sticks to prepare a fire to bake one last meal for herself and her son before they starved to death. Times were desperate. However, Elijah told her to fix him a meal with the meager supply she had left. She obeyed, and

God miraculously provided her a never-ending supply of flour and oil. Never hungry again!

Reading the story of the widow made me wonder: The widow, who evidently was a good person to be so generous to Elijah, was suffering because of the sins of Israel. Could some of my suffering be a result of others' sin and disobedience? Or was I in this place because of something I was doing wrong? The widow evidently asked those questions herself when her son died (after the miracle of the never-ending supply of oil and flour). She asked Elijah, "Have you come to me to bring my sin to remembrance, and to kill my son?" (v. 18). This was quite the houseguest she had on her hands. Yet God restored her son after Elijah prayed, and she was relieved: "I know that you are a man of God," she said (v. 24).

I couldn't get away from the fact that here I was, a follower of Jesus whose "yoke was easy and burden light," living with so much stress that I was in this much pain. I had thought I was zealous for God—I was trying to make a difference in the world. But something evidently was haywire. I wondered, *Is it just the world I'm living in? Or is it the result of disobedience in my own life?*

ELIJAH SEEMED TO THINK GOD'S WHOLE KINGDOM WAS HIS RESPONSIBILITY

In Elijah's day, there were those in Israel who believed in God as well as those who were into idol worship, even though it seems that Elijah wasn't aware of them. As I look back, I confess that I often had the attitude that if I didn't do it, it wouldn't get done. I still struggle with that feeling—that I have to make everyone in our family happy, be involved in ministry up to my eyebrows. But I did begin to realize that God has only called us to be faithful to our part. It is arrogant to assume that it's all on my shoulders.

There were, God reminded Elijah later in the desert, 7,000 people who had not bowed to Baal! In Elijah's mind, though, no one else was following God quite as intensely as he was. In fact, Obadiah, King Ahab's governor, risked Jezebel's wrath to hide one hundred of God's prophets in caves.

When Elijah brought all the people to a place for a showdown with the prophets of Baal, he confronted the people with the challenge, "How long are you going to waver between two opinions?" First Kings 18:21 says the people were completely silent. Just stared at him. I'm sure Elijah was thinking, *What does it take for these people to listen to God? Three years of drought and nothing—no response at all?* So he called them near so they could see how he repaired the altar of God. Perhaps the lesson was, "Okay, folks, back to basics."

And then Elijah had a major breakthrough after years of struggle. After Elijah repaired the altar, the fire of God came down and consumed the sacrifice and the wood, the stone—water, everything. It was a spectacular display of God's power, and the people finally realized that the Lord was God and began shouting, "The Lord is God!" Elijah cleaned house, spiritually speaking, and had all the prophets of Baal destroyed. The good news was that now God was sending rain, putting an end to the drought. The bad news was that

Queen Jezebel was furious with Elijah and swore that she would kill him, just as Elijah had destroyed the prophets of Baal. So just before it began to rain, Elijah ran for his life, running into the desert. He ran toward Mount Horeb, not being directed by God, only running to get away. He became exhausted. An angel fed him twice on the way, and when he got there, he stayed in a cave. God confronted Elijah in the desert twice with this question: "What are you doing here, Elijah?"

ELIJAH WAS EXHAUSTED, OVERWHELMED, AND SCARED

He just plain wanted to die. What was he doing there? He was worn out after his great victory and his marathon run to escape the wrath of Jezebel. After all he'd been through, trying to preach God's truth to an idolatrous nation, then finally seeing God's power convince the people to wholeheartedly come back to Him . . . after all that, he could think only about getting out of there. Escaping. I wonder if that isn't why we often end up in the desert after a great victory; or because we're afraid. It may be a distraction from pain or something in our lives, and we run, run, run, and find ourselves in a desert. And then God asks us, "What are you doing here?"

When finally Elijah was ready to hear God, it was through the still, small voice—which was as powerful as the mighty fire that consumed the altar in front of the prophets of Baal. And that's when God gave Elijah further marching orders—to go back and do some investing in the kingdom;

to see that the work of God would be carried out in succeeding generations. The big battle was won; now it was time to rebuild the kingdom.

ANSWERS IN THE DESERT

He will feed His flock like a shepherd;
He will gather the lambs with His arm,
And carry them in His bosom,
And gently lead those who are with young.

—ISAIAH 40:11

It was a defining moment in my life when I was confronted by the question *What am I doing here?* And I've come to believe that it is in the desert experiences where we can finally hear that question and respond to it. God will nourish us there and feed us with truth that we need to hear.

When our youngest son, Andy, was playing junior varsity basketball, he sometimes got to play the last minute of the varsity game. Bill and I tried to get to all of the games—especially the home games—but this particular night Andy's team was playing a school that was a six-hour drive from home and neither Bill nor I could go. That possible one minute of play was important—and we were missing it. The local radio station carried the game live, and we'd tuned in at home, even though the reception was bad. Other frequencies kept breaking in, and we could barely make sense of the play-by-play commentary.

At halftime, Bill and I looked at each other, grabbed the car keys, and said to Amy, who was eleven at the time, "Let's go!" As we drove the thirty minutes toward Redmond, where the radio station was based, the reception became clearer. Finally we could hear the game in all its glory.

We pulled off the highway onto a frontage road and parked among the juniper and sagebrush that populate the high desert. Leaning back, we listened for the Big Moment. Would Andy get in? Amy was convinced we had taken leave of our senses to drive out in the middle of nowhere to listen to a game, but she waited patiently with us.

With less than a minute to go, the announcer said, "And now number three for the Panthers, Andy Carmichael, checks into the game." Within that minute, Andy made a three-point basket! We hugged each other, jubilant. It was worth it! We had heard it! We had shared the moment and then headed home, satisfied.

As we drove, I thought about listening: How easy it is to hear but how difficult to listen. Real listening often happens best in the desert. Listening to what God is trying to get through to me is sometimes painful, and I may have to admit I was wrong. Real listening may bring me to the point, as I was to learn painfully, that my whole way of thinking and living needed to change. My practical theology had to change.

Scripture says God was not in the great wind, earthquake, or fire on the mountaintop, but afterward, God spoke in a gentle whisper—a still, small voice. How we say we long to hear God! But where is the place that He speaks? Where is the place to hear Him clearly, without interference? When things are going well, we don't listen so intently. And like the experience of Elijah, those rare, wonderful times when we do hear Him most often come when we're prepared for them in the desert—in pain, sitting under a scrubby juniper tree, wondering what on earth we're doing here, knowing only that we need to hear God.

"It is," W. H. Auden says, "where we are wounded that God speaks to us." None of us like the wounded places. But that is where life is stripped of its distractions, the constant interferences. It is a place to listen. And it is a place to respond.

How to Hear God

In *Signposts*, A. W. Tozer wrote:

> Retire from the world each day to some private spot, even if it be only the bedroom. Stay in the secret place till the surrounding noises begin to fade out of your heart and a sense of God's presence envelops you. Deliberately tune out the unpleasant sounds and come out of your closet determined not to hear them. Listen for the inward Voice till you learn to recognize it. Stop trying to compete with others. Give yourself

to God and then be what and who you are without regard to what others think. Learn to pray inwardly every moment. After a while, you can do this even while you work. Practice candor, childlike honesty, humility. Pray for a single eye. Read less, but read what is important to your inner life. Never let your mind remain scattered for very long. Call home your roving thoughts. Gaze on Christ with the eyes of your soul. Practice spiritual concentration.[2]

The desert offers you an opportunity to ask, What am I living that I believe? Perhaps more than anything, the desert is a crisis of belief, an opportunity to reaffirm what we truly believe.

Jesus said in Mark 8:17–18, "Do you not yet perceive nor understand? Is your heart still hardened? Having eyes, do you not see? And having ears, do you not hear?" We need not fear truth because the truth will set us free.

Often the "real agenda" does not get put on our calendars: time alone with God . . . study of His Word. We are busy, we are distracted. But when we are in a desert experience, we are reminded of what is most important. In our quiet time with God in the desert, we can truly listen; obey; then become. James 1:22 encourages us to be "doers of the word and not hearers only." It is not enough to hear; we must obey what we hear.

PRAYING FOR RAIN: GOD'S INTERVENTION

Then Elijah said to Ahab, "Go up, eat and drink; for there is the sound of abundance of rain."

—1 KINGS 18:41

We need water in the desert to keep us alive. Up on the north bench of Montana east of the Rockies where we lived and where my brother now farms, it seems that you can see forever. We could see the clouds rolling over the mountains toward us, some with rain and some that billowed on by, and there were many times we literally prayed for rain, longed for it. Our very survival depended on the crops getting enough moisture at the right time. I never saw my dad happier than in late spring when the crops were up, and we would begin to have a good, soaking rain. Rain. He'd come into the house, a grin on his face, his blue eyes sparkling. He'd suggest to my mother, "Let's drive up to the mountains."

My desert experience made me long for, pray for, God's intervention—more so than at any other time. Like the survival of our crops, it seemed that my survival depended upon God's intervention. I could not go on as I was; I needed a sovereign God's intervention.

My husband and I have found the best way to renew our love is to take time to get away together. Away from the

15

pressures of life and without the distractions, we are able to hear one another again, see one another, listen to one another. Yes, it can be painful sometimes to hear the hard truths we need to hear, the ones we don't have time for in the crush of life; but within the protected shelter of listening and acceptance, love is renewed.

And so it is with our relationship with God. At times He uses the desert as a set-apart place in our lives to speak peace, truth, and love to us. In the book of Hosea, He said,

Behold, I will allure her,
Will bring her into the wilderness,
And speak comfort to her.
I will give her her vineyards from there,
And the Valley of Achor as a door of hope;
She shall sing there,
As in the days of her youth,
As in the day when she came up from the land of Egypt.
And it shall be, in that day . . .
That you will call Me "My Husband." (2:14–16)

As I waited on God, journaled, and read Scripture, I realized I'd been running, too, like Elijah. My days had been filled with so many activities—many of them good, but many mindless. When I finally stopped to listen, I realized that there were some deep losses that I had not taken the time to grieve. My method had been to keep a stiff upper lip, keep going, deny the pain, deny the loss. But finally I was ready to stop and listen.

— REFLECTION —

Read the story of Elijah's desert experience in 1 Kings 17, 18, and 19. What had to happen before Elijah gave God his full attention? Is there a time in your life that you could relate to Elijah's situation? What have you learned about hearing God's voice?

— PRAYER —

Speak, Lord, for Your servant hears. Grant me ears to hear, eyes to see, a will to obey, a heart to love; then declare what You will; reveal what You will; command what You will. Amen.

—CHRISTINA ROSSETTI, *Little Book of Prayers*

2

THE DESERT OF LOSS

I have been afflicted and ready to die from my
   youth . . .
I am distraught . . .
Loved one and friend You have put far from me,
And my acquaintances into darkness.

—Psalm 88:15, 18

— SUGGESTED READING: THE BOOK OF RUTH —

My journey into the desert took some time, although I wasn't aware that it was closing around me, hitting me full force by 1985. I believe the seeds for it were planted six years earlier with a significant loss—the death of my father. Also, my mother was having chemotherapy for cancer at the same time that my father was dying. I thought somehow I needed to be strong for her and so swallowed my tears for my father, even doing the music for both of my father's funerals—one in Oregon and the final one at our Montana home. "Daddy's not dead," I wrote rather grandly in my journal. "He's alive now more than the rest of us. He's just not here." Which is true with eyes of faith, but it shows my state of mind—I was denying the real pain of a very real loss.

I worried over my mother's fragile condition. Mother was extremely important in my life—more like a close friend. How could I bear to live without her, too? I became consumed with the thought that if I somehow had a daughter, she would fill the hole my mother would leave when I lost her. Since we were unable to have any more biological children, I latched onto the idea of adopting a daughter. I rationalized, "There are many motherless daughters; and I need a daughter—so it's logical—we'll adopt." As I look back now I realize that I was trying to protect myself from the pain of loss, to get insurance against life: brick by brick, piece by piece, building the perfect life that threatened to eventually crush me.

And then my mother did the unthinkable—she, too, left us. It was on a warm, sweet June morning. My sisters and I drove the few blocks from the home where our mother had been, leaving hurriedly so as not to see the undertaker take Mom away. Some scenes would be too unbearable, we reasoned. My sister was staying in a motor home parked next to my other sister's house that final week of Mom's life, and as I went inside with her, I accidentally smashed my thumb in the door. Ouch. I held a bag of ice to it, somehow relieved to have physical pain as well as an emotional one.

Everything seemed strange, surreal. The enormous sense of relief all mixed up with grief; the many phone calls to make; the decisions about the funeral. My brothers to call, my children. Trying unsuccessfully to contact my husband, who was somewhere in Alaska on a speaking engagement. Longing suddenly now to be home. Desperately longing to to be with my children. Hug the dogs. Sweep the kitchen floor. Sleep in my own bed. Call Mother, and tell her what I am going through . . . I catch myself, reminded of what this is. It is her death—and it is final. I feel the hollow ache of not having Mother to call—and she's not there to listen, to say it's going to be all right, because the hurt is losing her.

I smashed my thumbnail right at the base; it hurt fiercely, and somehow I was glad. I was wounded, and I could prove it by looking at it. The damaged part of my nail eventually grew out, and after I trimmed it off weeks later it began to look normal again; no one even knew I'd smashed my thumb. And later, after Mother's funeral, life would get back to normal. To look at me, you would think the wound was gone, but the pain would still be there, inside. And it still is, although it is true that time dulls the pain. But death, the final enemy that separates loved ones forever on this earth, can lead us into a desert experience where we're left wondering, *Why do we have to lose people we love so much?*

Earlier that week, I'd sat by Mother's bed, thinking there

was something very familiar about the process, and it seemed in many ways like a birth. Pain, uncertainty, travail. Knowing her departure was imminent, yet not knowing when. Days seemed like years as we kept vigil near her bedside, and we children came and went, watching her decline hourly. In those final days, there were some sweet moments; some smiles, even laughter. But watching her die, and trying to make her comfortable as she left us, was heart-wrenching.

Finally the struggle was over, and time as she knew it—minutes, days, months, years—stopped. At ten 'til five on a Tuesday morning, my sister, who was doing night duty, called me: "Mom's with Jesus . . ." I got there in just a few minutes and knelt by her bed, cradled her little frame that was still warm but so still. And so that week we made the trek back to Montana to her final resting place here on earth, and laying her beside Dad under the headstone that reads, "Till He Comes . . ." After losing both my mother and my father, it struck me that even though I was all grown up, I was now an orphan.

Later I wrote in my journal:

> *Mother died three weeks ago. I write that line, but it is still so hard to believe. How can she die? That woman of laughter, of music? Of poetry and quick wit—unfailing arms of love and acceptance? Even in her declining state, she loved. How can we say it is better for her? She is gone! Gone from us. But present to God, to loved ones on the other side. Surely it must be so. Death cannot still one so vibrant, so lovely. I keep trying*

to burn the memory of her laughter, the sound of her voice, the warmth of her smile deep into my mind so I won't forget. I wonder, "When you lose someone you love . . . someone who loves you . . . what happens to the love? Where does it go?"

INSIGHTS FROM RUTH AND NAOMI

The book of Ruth—only four chapters long—is a wonderful story of love and loss and second chances. In it we see how Naomi handled her losses and we can gain insights from how she and Ruth were eventually restored.

When Naomi came back home to Bethlehem, the people hardly recognized her. "It's Naomi," the neighbors whispered. "No," she contradicted harshly. "Call me Mara—meaning bitter—because I went out full and I've come back empty."

How did Naomi get to that place of bitter grief? She had started out with high hopes as she married Elimelech. Naomi and Elimelech's family was from Bethlehem, where hundreds of years later Jesus would be born. They were a well-known and respected family and eventually had two little boys: Mahlon and Chilion. However, there was a famine in the land and times were hard. So as a resilient young family, they left to go to Moab where there was opportunity.

And then the head of their family, Elimelech, died. Naomi arranged to have her two sons married off to Orpah and Ruth, local women. And then, tragically, within ten years of marriage both her sons died, too, not leaving any children.

Naomi's losses were piling up: First, Naomi had moved far away from her beloved home; then her husband died; and then both her sons died, leaving no grandchildren. To her, that had to be the worst imaginable—complete devastation, complete loss. In those days, the extinction of the family line was unthinkable, and Naomi was facing that loss.

NAOMI FACED HER GRIEF SQUARELY

She took time to grieve. She wept as she saw her losses. It's healthy to grieve, to take time to acknowledge the anger. Depression often happens when anger is turned inward or unexpressed. When a major loss happens, we often react with the "why's." But God can handle our questions while He patiently loves us through the process. The good news to remember is that Jesus said, "In the world you will have tribulation; but be of good cheer, I have overcome the world" (John 16:33).

NAOMI LOOKED FOR GOOD NEWS

She heard the famine at home was over. This may have taken her awhile, but she eventually decided to do something. Naomi had to make plans; there were probably a lot of loose ends and unanswered questions, but she persevered.

NAOMI TOOK ACTION

Naomi decided to return. She used some assertiveness, made some constructive choices with her own life. At first, her two daughters-in-law both said they would go with her.

After all, they had experienced loss, too. It was when Naomi actually took steps to go back to Bethlehem that her healing began. She didn't wait until she "felt" whole, "felt" full—she took steps.

NAOMI UNSELFISHLY CONSIDERED ORPAH AND RUTH

In the midst of Naomi's grief, she realized there were other people hurting, too. She realized her daughters-in-law were young—there was no need for them to go with her. There was still time for them to remarry, have children. She told each of them, "Go back to your mother's house." In other words, "I can't supply you with another husband. Get on with your life." Orpah finally agreed and kissed Naomi good-bye. But Ruth clung to Naomi. Stubborn Ruth!

NAOMI WAS CONFRONTED AGAIN
BY GRIEF AS SHE RETURNED HOME

Grief happens again and again. That's the way losses are. As she returned home to Bethlehem, loss hit Naomi once more as she saw the old familiar places where she and Elimelech had such high hopes, where their two sons played—now all gone. Her old friends came out to meet her and asked, "Is this Naomi?" Evidently she'd aged. Life had not been kind to her. Grief can come in cycles, abruptly intruding at the most unexpected times.

NAOMI WAS ANGRY AT GOD

She lashed out, "He did this to me! The Almighty's hand

is against me. Don't call me Naomi [meaning 'pleasant']; call me Mara [meaning 'bitter']."

Anger is a natural part of grieving, and God can handle our anger. But it's important to acknowledge it and then go on.

NAOMI'S HEALING BEGAN AS SHE GOT CAUGHT UP IN CYCLES, SEASONS OF LIFE

Harvest was on, and she got involved through Ruth. The seasons, the natural rhythms of life will help heal us if we allow them to help. Life does go on and will help carry us through unbearable times.

NAOMI INVESTED IN RUTH

She began caring for someone besides herself. Naomi became interested in life again and advised Ruth on how to pursue Boaz. The point of this is that in the midst of our own losses, we must never stop investing in people. Naomi began to forge new relationships and new loyalties, and renewed old ones.

FULFILLMENT WAS RESTORED TO NAOMI THROUGH NEW LIFE

Ruth and Boaz were married and had a baby boy they named Obed. They brought him to Naomi, asking her to care for him, and Naomi's arms were once again full. It's interesting to realize that the name Obed means "serving." It is often through giving to others that we receive fulfillment and healing.

THE RESTORATION OF RUTH AND NAOMI TOOK TIME

It didn't happen instantly. The loss of a spouse is enormously deep. I can barely comprehend it after watching three of my close friends as they have tried to work through this life-changing, catastrophic loss. A friend who lost her husband of nearly thirty years told me there were many times when standing at the kitchen sink or driving in a car, she'd suddenly feel off-balance and wonder: *Who am I? I'm not a wife anymore. Where do I fit? Where do I sit on Sunday in church? What do I do evenings? What is my life now? I'm lost.*

Sometimes in our losses it takes time to see the living, the positive. And there are times, as for Naomi, when it seems that the losses pile up. Losses are an inevitable part of life, but it doesn't make them any easier. The good news is that we often meet God in our most difficult places, our places of loss and of disappointment. Isaiah said, "In the year that King Uzziah died, I saw the Lord" (Isa. 6:1). When we lose people or things we can become comforted because He can become our everything.

. . . Christianity is Christ living in us, and Christ has conquered everything . . . His love is so much stronger than death that the death of a Christian is a kind of triumph. And although we rightly sorrow . . . we rejoice in their death because it proves to us the strength of our mutual love. This is our great inheritance . . . this grip of clean love that holds us so fast that it keeps us eternally free. This love, this life, this presence, is the witness that the spirit of Christ lives in us, and that we belong to Him, and that the Father has given us to Him, and no man shall snatch us out of His hand.

—THOMAS MERTON, *No Man Is an Island*[1]

NOW WHAT?

In dealing with loss, three things are essential:

1. *Be honest about your losses and grieve.* Talk it over with someone; let the tears flow; journal your thoughts, your pain. Acknowledge the loss. When you take time to grieve, you are honoring what or whom you have lost. It's been said that all neuroses are substitutes for legitimate suffering. In order to avoid being neurotic, you must pay attention to the loss; you must grieve it before you can move on.

2. *Allow God into that place of pain and receive His comfort.* Read scriptures that minister to your deepest need and accept them into your spirit. What does one do in this place of "bereavement," this desert of loss? It is a place to pour one's whole self out to God.

3. *Invest in the future.* Take stock of your life; investigate to see what still remains, and then strengthen it. Look to renew old dreams and make new plans. Be creative in turning your loss into gain. On both my parents' birthdays, I do something to honor their memory. For instance, one year on my dad's birthday (because he was so good at caring for

people), I did a project to help a family in need. These intentional acts can help bring healing.

Flora Wuellner writes eloquently about joy and pain:

> It is significant that the suffering to which God invites us always includes joy along with the pain and always brings with it the authentic awareness of growth and deepened love as part of its intrinsic nature . . . Strangely enough, it is often hard to face the fact that we are suffering. Sometimes the pain is so chronic that we have grown accustomed to it. Sometimes we are numbed and anesthetized. Sometimes we have pushed ourselves so quickly into a positive response that we do not allow ourselves to feel the pain. Perhaps we try too quickly to forgive and forget or feel that our suffering is trivial or that we have no right to register suffering. Often it is with a sense of shock that we realize we are grieving and that we may have been carrying unhealed wounds for a long time. This often happens with those in the helping professions who are so used to themselves in the role of comforter and supporter that they become unaware of their own feelings and needs.[2]

‹◊›

How else but through a broken heart
May Lord Christ enter in?

—OSCAR WILDE, *The Ballad of Reading Gaol* (1898)

‹◊›

THE DIFFERENT FACES OF LOSS

It was in the desert of my own losses that it became clear to me that ultimately, life was out of my control, and the illusion that things were going according to schedule popped like a soap bubble. Big losses, small losses, piled up one after the other as they do so often in midlife. Besides the deaths of my parents, my children began leaving home (as they should); then I lost my position with the magazines, something I'd poured my energy into for years. I felt that I was standing on the seashore and the sea was eroding the earth beneath me.

I felt guilt in experiencing pain for some of those losses, because they shouldn't seem like losses . . . they were just changes, weren't they? And yet loss wears different faces. While some losses are painful and hard to reconcile, others are simply part of moving through life. Change. Sometimes it happens without our wanting it. Sometimes it doesn't happen when we wish it would. A Greek proverb says, "There is nothing permanent except change."[3]

Good things can also be losses because to have one thing, we lose another. Children being born; going off to school; moving to a new place; friendship changes. But when we hold on too long to something that needs to change, it can be our undoing. After all, our hands can only hold so much. There is a time to let go, to move gracefully through life.

It is hard to let go, especially of our children. I remember my mother saying right after my brother and sister and I left for school within three years: "I feel bereft of my children." *Bereft*—it has the same root word as *bereavement*.

CHILDREN LEAVING HOME

God, they're leaving . . . one at a time! How can You expect us parents to be so involved and then just check out, like dandelion seeds blowing in the wind? Lord, thank You for allowing me to be a steward of such beautiful children, who are, of course, Yours. It is hard to love them so much and let go all at the same time. Show me how to love them in new, liberating ways that will free them to be all they can be. I release them . . . again, into Your care. In Christ's name, amen.

Today a yellow school bus full of children passed the house and I was unexpectedly hit with a sense of loss as I looked out the window. This is the first September that I have not gotten school supplies . . . school clothes. How quickly those years went.

I clearly remember the day that our firstborn son, Jon, came into my office after he had received his acceptance to college and wanted to talk. He worked as a lifeguard that summer and I remember thinking how handsome and healthy he looked, and my mind flashed back to his first day of school—how infinitely precious he looked with his white-blond hair, sporting a new navy blue jacket and jeans as he held his pencil box with new crayons and pencils inside. And now here he was, another big step.

I wondered how I could wake up ordinary mornings and not have him sitting at the kitchen bar eating breakfast, excited about what he was going to do that day. And yet he was so eager to go, how could I not encourage him? His eyes were full of hope, dreams, promises, and confidence. *Hang on to it, Jonny,* I remember thinking. *Only you won't, entirely.* The flawless beauty of youth is so fragile, such an illusion.

I remembered being his age, packing for college in southern California. When I hugged my father good-bye he began to weep, which literally shocked me into a sober silence (I was wailing myself). It never occurred to me that my parents might feel pain at the separation. And now I feel the pain. *Serves me right,* I thought. *My son leaving me.* It's natural, it's right, but there's pain in the tearing. Jon's leaving home was only the beginning of a gradual procession of our children moving away from home, moving on into their own lives.

Just this year Amy, our youngest of five, left home to try her wings. While I know it's good for her and I wouldn't change it, somehow I don't want it to be over. I like kids coming home from school, throwing their books on the table, yelling, "Hi, Mom!" I like the fragrance of warm cookies filling the house and having to say, "Just one! Dinner's almost ready." *I like being a mom.*

Emptiness has connotations of once having been full. I suppose the *empty nest* is a classic example, although that doesn't really describe our house. Our house is not empty. We have people coming and going—adult children, grandchildren, relatives. Both my husband's and my offices are in our home. But what is changing is our relationship with our children, as they seem to be moving farther and farther away, geographically as well as emotionally. All good, all natural, yes. But the "hands-on" shaping and parenting are over. And I have to admit—it's a big loss for me. What I have felt empty from is purpose. Being a mother was all I wanted to do and be as I was growing up. Now with this change, it feels as if I'm left standing at the open door, watching them leave, asking, *Do you have to go so soon? You mean it's over?*

And yet in the "emptiness," my husband and I are finding more room for each other and realizing in a fresh way how important we are to each other and that we should not take each other for granted. We are now seeing each other more. We are sensing a new freedom, a new focus, but often until we are forced into an "empty" place, we cannot see new opportunities.

Change helps us to grow as we are confronted by asking ourselves: *Where is my security? In another person, a title, a position? In what I do?* Outward changes can facilitate inward changes that make us rely more and more on our ultimate source of Living Water, Christ Jesus.

After Loss

My husband and I had a magazine company for twelve years. It was a family adventure; we were all involved. Bill did the business and marketing; I was involved editorially. We used our children for photo shoots, and I helped fix some of the food for the shoots. I wrote about our children in a column. The staff was like our extended family. The magazines had been our purpose, our platform. So while we were willingly looking forward to releasing some of the responsibilities, it was also a loss that we didn't fully comprehend when we first began the transaction. It was only later that we realized what a big change it was for us. Bill was no longer "president," with a staff at his command. I was no longer an "editor," with a connection to readers about whom I was passionate and felt a connection, an identity.

So when changes are finally made, sometimes it takes a while to assimilate the loss; to realize there's an empty place. You are left with a sense of just going through the motions — get groceries, do chores, pay bills, watch TV. ("Is that all there is?") The rest of life looks like a long, straight road ahead with nothing in sight. Is this the abundant life? The well of life that springs up? I look deep inside and cannot even see my own reflection.

The desert seems to be a consequence of loss, or even change. Perhaps we women are more susceptible (although men suffer, too), but we tend to define ourselves by our relationships. We are mother, wife, daughter, sister. Men are more apt to define themselves by their work. It doesn't seem fair that one of the first questions men are asked when making an acquaintance is, "What do you do?" And yet it is true that men often are defined by what they do. Although women are defined by their relationships, what we "do" can be very life-defining as well.

When our oldest son, Jon, left for college, at first the family seemed violated. But life adjusted some and then went on, although we were aware that Jon's leaving was just the beginning. It is an awesome thing to be a parent. Your heart is almost without question given away, divided among the children, and they aren't even conscious of it. It's only later, when you watch your own parent stop breathing, that you realize something incredibly important is gone. Somehow I think the losses of my mother and father and my children leaving home were all bound up together. What changed forever was my role as a daughter; as an at-home mother.

Lord, you have been our dwelling place throughout
    all generations.
Before the mountains were born
    or you brought forth the earth and the world,
    from everlasting to everlasting you are God.

—PSALM 90:1–2 NIV

GIVING OUT OF LOSS

I walked a mile with Pleasure,
She chattered all the way;
But left me none the wiser
As she went on her way.
I walked a mile with Sorrow;

And not a word said she,
But O, the things I learned
When sorrow walked with me.

—ROBERT BROWNING HAMILTON

———————————— ‹◇› ————————————

What does loss do for us? It gives us many gifts that we would not have otherwise: honesty, compassion, appreciation for others. The realization that we must take time to express important things *now*. It can make us better people.

Many of us who have experienced losses can remember unfeeling or hurtful things people said to us at the time. They meant well, but when we are hurting, we are vulnerable to comments. When we experience loss, we know better how to identify with or relate to someone.

I've learned that it's essential to take time to see all of life—the joys and sorrows, the sweet and the bitter, and to accept the comfort that God offers through others. New places can be scary, but remember, He is there—because He is the same yesterday, today, and forever.

All that we commit to Him is safe. All. Our hopes, our dreams, our fears, the people we love so much, the people who have hurt us and disappointed us—everything. Martin Luther, who had many losses, said, "I have held many things in my hand and I've lost them all, but that which I have committed to God, I still have." Much has changed in the world since then, and yet some things have

36

not changed. We, too, live in challenging times, and although we have material things and opportunity, there is much to distract us from following Christ, from believing. Os Guinness wrote, "We have too much to live with and not enough to live for."[4] In the desert of loss, we are given the opportunity to truly grasp what we are living for and believe in the unchanging God.

Do not look forward to the changes and chances of this life in fear; rather look to them with full hope that, as they arise, God, whose you are, will deliver you out of them. He is your keeper. He has kept you hitherto. Do you but hold fast to his dear hand, and he will lead you safely through all things; and, when you cannot stand, he will bear you in his arms. Do not look forward to what may happen tomorrow. Our Father will either shield you from suffering, or he will give you strength to bear it.

—ST. FRANCIS OF SALES[5]

— REFLECTION —

Think back on the last ten years of your life, and note any significant changes: a death in the family; children leaving home; a change in jobs; or a move. Read the book of Ruth and consider how she and Naomi handled their losses. What can you learn from them that could be applied to your own life?

— PRAYER —

Lord, when I see a door closing behind me, let me not be fearful. Your promise is sure: You will open another door, making a way for me in what looks like an impossible wilderness. Thank You for the power that turns deserts into rivers of blessing. . . Amen.

—CATHERINE MARSHALL,
My Personal Prayer Diary[6]

Blessed are they that mourn: for they shall be comforted.

—MATTHEW 5:4 KJV

3

THE DESERT OF PAIN

Have I sinned? What have I done to you, O watcher
of all humanity? Why have you made me your target?

—Job 7:20 NLT

— SUGGESTED READING: THE BOOK OF JOB —

PAIN IS A THIEF

Pain robs you of concentration, focus. When you're in
its grips, forget noble thoughts and creative plans
because all you can think about is getting relief. Forget even
reading, because the pain—if it's intense—can consume you.
It's true that Job in the Bible had incredible losses—his children, his property. But it was when he became covered with
boils that things got really ugly. That's when he wanted to die.

I'd always been a healthy, active person until my immune

system took a jolt when I had toxic shock syndrome several years ago. I recovered initially, but after that, it seemed I couldn't get well. A year, then two years passed, and I still had frequent low-grade fevers; chronic pain in my joints; mind-numbing fatigue. It seemed I hurt all the time, although I couldn't tell you exactly where. The degenerating disks in my back were also giving me problems, and I had surgery to alleviate the pain. Along with the pain was a depression that seemed to have a paralyzing grip on me. It was some time later that I was to learn that physical and emotional pain are often related.

After my trip to the Mayo Clinic, during which I had been given a clean bill of health and was told that I needed most of all to deal with the stress in my life, I had an accident. It was our last day of vacation, and we were boating in the San Juan Islands off the Washington coast. School started in a few days, and we were ready to go home. Bill angled the boat toward the dock, and being a good first mate, I poised to jump off and tie up.

As I stepped off the boat, my foot slipped off the dock and I kept going, falling into the cold ocean. I remember it as if it were a dream in slow motion happening to someone else. One thought was uppermost—not to go under the boat, to avoid hitting the prop. I grabbed onto a railing of the boat as it slammed me against the dock, and somehow Bill and the kids got the boat stopped and helped me clamber out, where I lay moaning in pain. I had bruises and scrapes, and later, X-rays showed a fractured and dislocated shoulder as well as a couple of herniated disks in my neck. The doctor said he'd seen only one other person with an injury like this—a rodeo bronc rider!

I have given birth four times, but I have to say, I have never had such pain, ever. But after surgery and months of physical therapy, I was better, almost as good as new. And then I lifted a box of books the wrong way. Suddenly, the pain was back, gripping me in its vise, affecting my neck, arm, and shoulder. Back to physical therapy I went, the doctor talking surgery again. The physical therapist told me that besides lifting wrong, I'd been holding my head wrong as I walked and sat. She told me if I even move my head forward a couple of inches, I add pounds to my frame. Well, I did finally have another surgery and the pain has subsided now, but I know what not to do to make it flare up again.

IS THERE ANYTHING REDEMPTIVE IN PAIN?

Concerning this [thorn in the flesh] I pleaded with the Lord three times that it might depart from me. And He said to me, "My grace is sufficient for you, for My strength is made perfect in weakness."

—2 CORINTHIANS 12:8–9

Pain is a great leveler; an eloquent reminder of our humanity. Paul the apostle had a thorn in his side that he prayed three times to have removed, but God didn't see fit to remove it. But Paul received something even better—a revelation of God's grace and strength in his weakness. Without his "thorn in the flesh," whatever it was, he'd never have known God's strength as he did. When you think about it, that's pretty redemptive.

In my recuperation, the Psalms came alive for me. One day I wrote in my journal from my bed:

Time to count blessings, my soul. Time to "forget not all His benefits," my soul. Look around you, see how blessed you are with family, friends, comforts. So you're in pain. So are many people in the world, many in far worse pain than you. (Why does this fact not comfort me? I hurt. I miss being with my husband. I'm tired of this bed, tired of watching people come and go. I'm frustrated by looking at a messy house and dirty windows, unable to do anything about it.) Sometimes in the quiet I hear that still voice: "He leads me beside still waters. He restores my soul . . ." Lord, thank You for reminding me that You are in control.

He who learns must suffer. And even in our sleep pain that cannot forget falls drop by drop upon the heart, and in our own despair, against our will, comes wisdom to us by the awful grace of God.

—AESCHYLUS, 456 B.C.

ONE FAMILY'S HOLOCAUST

To tell the truth, I struggle with this chapter because I know some wonderful people who literally have gone through holocausts of loss and pain and disease. How can mere words even begin to describe them? But there are some things that we know apply in even the worst losses: God is real; He loves us. There is a plan, although we can't see it all now. And we can fulfill His law by loving one another.

Several of us met one day at the home of a friend to talk about our desert experiences and what we'd learned from them. We all had different stories: One woman was suffering from chronic depression; another, a successful professional, had lived a quiet life of disappointment and despair with an emotionally wounded husband; one woman, an artist, felt much misunderstood and alienated by the Christian community. She was also struggling with the fact that her daughter had just told her she was a lesbian. Another woman in our group was dealing with the loss of her cherished home through a business deal.

But I was most struck with Amy's story. She was not feeling well that day, but of all of us, she seemed to radiate peace as she told her story. She was blessed, she said, to marry her best friend, Larry. And although they went through the pain of realizing they were infertile, over time God gave them a wonderful daughter through adoption. And then their lives seemed to go from a productive, happy situation to one of physical deterioration. Larry's juvenile diabetes began to spiral out of control, and as his condition worsened, he had to have kidney dialysis. He was able to get a kidney and pancreatic transplant, but that didn't slow the disease and Larry was in a coma for two months. When he woke up, his leg was gone, amputated because of the ravages of the disease. "Of course by this time, he couldn't work and had to be on disability," Amy told us: "Our focus changed completely."

And then another bombshell: Amy discovered she had advanced ovarian cancer. She said, "Illness changes people, but I'm hanging on to God with everything I have." Although the prognosis for Amy was not good, she said, "Within the body of Christ, I feel so loved. It's so humbling. I've had to learn to receive. I've learned that when I'm down physically, I'm up spiritually. God is letting me know He's not through with me. And I want to know the purpose for this!"

Not long after our meeting, Amy went to be with Jesus. Recently, I spoke to her mother, who told me how the family has pulled together to love and care for one another. Larry's health has improved, and he is taking initiative in caring for his daughter. With the help of the rest of the family, all of them are overwhelmed by the love and care shown them by others through this difficult time. Even in the most painful of times, love has triumphed.

THE PAIN OF THOSE CLOSE TO US

In many ways it's harder to be with someone who is in pain—either physically or emotionally—than to be in pain oneself. We want to fix it, and when we can't, we feel help-less and uncomfortable. During the time I was struggling with my health, my chronic pain was hard on Bill. He is the kind of man who can fix anything—or tries to—but he couldn't fix me. Watching me in pain made him angry, frus-trated, and worried.

Neva, a friend of mine, believes she has spent a lifetime in the "desert" by being married to a man with deep emo-tional pain from early childhood wounds. They had several children, and she did not feel she could be released from the marriage. In the early years of their marriage, she hoped he would somehow get over those wounds. But he didn't, and she learned that she could not fix them. "So instead," she said, "I learned to grow deep in the Word." Neva went on to say, "I've come to realize that God is not so much interested in my happiness as in my holiness." She said that Paul the apos-tle's example and writings were a source of inspiration: Although Paul was imprisoned, he still had joy. Although Neva's marriage has often felt like a prison to her, she's learned to have joy in it and learned to give, learned to enjoy her sons, learned to enjoy life just where she is.

When we adopted our three-and-a-half-year-old daugh-ter from Korea, I had no idea of the inner pain that can come to one who has been abandoned. When Amy was six years old, Bill and I were leaving to go on a weekend speaking engagement. Although her grandparents and four older brothers were going to be there, she began acting up, jump-ing up and down on my bed, deliberately messing up things

I had laid out for the trip. I sternly corrected her, then went into the kitchen to serve dinner. She followed me, grabbed her place setting off the table, and put it back on the counter. Her little face was a storm cloud. I was about to lose my patience when I realized something was deeply troubling her.

I got down on the floor where she was sitting and took her in my arms and looked into her dark eyes. "Amy," I said softly, "what is wrong?"

She threw her arms around me and burst into sobs. "Don't leave me, Mommy! Please don't leave me!" My heart broke because I knew her vulnerability to being "left." I felt helpless, not knowing what to offer except my assurances, again. How could I convince her, how could I make her know I would never abandon her? I sat down with her and took her in my arms, and couldn't help my own tears. Suddenly Amy looked up at me, surprised. "Hey—why are you crying?" she asked.

"Amy, I feel sad because you are sad. But I promise you I will never stop being your mother, and I will love you, always."

"Oh, Mom, I love you, too!" She kissed me and jumped up and ran off to play, all smiles. As I sat on the floor and tried to figure out what that was all about, I realized that it was by my tears and my arms that Amy knew I cared, that I had identified with her feelings. That was a healing moment in her life, a growing step in believing she was wanted and loved. She seemed relieved that someone understood how she felt. This experience reminds me that our High Priest, Jesus, literally "got down" where we lived, and became

46

human, and He is touched by the feeling of our infirmities. By His nail-scarred hands, He proved His love for us.

When Amy was in her teens, there was a time when she literally cut herself on her arms—because, she said, it helped to somehow relieve the pain that was inside. Nothing ever made me feel more distraught than to know my daughter whom I loved so deeply was feeling such great pain . . . yet I was helpless to help her. We found that we needed to reach out and ask for help with Amy's pain, and there were many times we just held her and prayed. She is just now coming to a place of healing and peace at the age of twenty. If it is true that the Lord is near to those with a broken heart, maybe the place of brokenness is a good place to be as we just stay close to Him in that place.

For we do not have a High Priest who cannot sympathize with our weaknesses, but was in all points tempted as we are, yet without sin. Let us therefore come boldly to the throne of grace, that we may obtain mercy and find grace to help in time of need.

—HEBREWS 4:15–16

WHAT WE CAN LEARN FROM JOB

This is an amazing, ancient story of a good man set in the time of the patriarchs—Abraham, Isaac, and Jacob. There is much wisdom in the book of Job, and I suggest you read it thoughtfully, especially if you are in a time of suffering. Job loved God and his family and stayed away from evil, yet he lost everything. He had seven sons, three daughters, and many possessions, and was a spiritual leader among his children and the community.

Then there came a day when the sons of God came to present themselves before the Lord, and Satan came, too. The Lord asked Satan where he had come from, and Satan answered, "From going to and fro on the earth, and from walking back and forth on it." The Lord said to Satan, "Have you considered My servant Job, that there is none like him on the earth, a blameless and upright man?" (1:7–8).

Satan told God, "Of course Job loves and honors You! Look how You've blessed him. But if everything he has is taken away, he will curse You to Your face."

Then God did an astounding thing: He gave Satan permission to do anything to Job except lay a hand on him.

And that's when Job's problems began, one after the other: An invading army raided Job's oxen and killed many of his servants . . . then a fire destroyed more servants and the sheep . . . then another army came and killed the camels and other servants. A great wind came and destroyed the house where his sons and daughters were having a feast, killing them all. The rest of the story is Job's response to his suffering. He has three "friends" who show up to try to help him make sense of it, and finally Job has an encounter with God Himself. What can we learn from Job?

THERE ARE TIMES WE HAVE
NO IDEA WHY WE'RE SUFFERING

Job was not in on the conversation between God and Satan. He had no idea why he had all those losses. But his response was that he bowed down and worshiped. He recognized the hand of God—He gives; He takes away. We may never on this earth understand why some things happen.

WE ARE VULNERABLE TO PEOPLE'S COMMENTS
WHEN WE ARE IN THE MIDST OF PAIN

It is essential to stay in the Word to know what we know. It's also a good reminder to be careful what we say to other people who are in the midst of a holocaust. Sometimes saying nothing—or a sincere "I'm so sorry"—is the best. Well-meaning people at times feel compelled to make sense of senseless things. I remember standing next to my father's coffin, wondering why; and a man remarked to me, "I'm so glad your dad is with the Lord." I looked up and nodded, but inside I was crying, *Well, I'm not! I want him here with us!*

JOB COMPLAINED ABOUT HIS PAIN—
LOUD AND LONG—YET HE DID NOT BLAME GOD

After Job "vented," he declared: "Though He slay me, yet will I trust Him" (13:15). However, Job didn't get to this place of faith right away. He did a lot of questioning, agonizing. And then he spoke directly to God (13:20–23):

Only two things do not do to me,

Then I will not hide myself from You:

Withdraw Your hand far from me,

And let not the dread of You make me afraid.

Then call, and I will answer;

Or let me speak, then You respond to me . . . .

Make me know my transgression.

GOD ULTIMATELY REVEALED HIMSELF TO JOB

Chapters 38 through 41 of the book of Job contain a thundering, dramatic declaration from God as He presented His credentials as Creator of heaven and earth in vivid detail. Job was left speechless and humbled, and he finally responded, "Behold, I am vile . . . Now I see . . . Now I hear. I repent."

I read these last four chapters of Job on the Oregon coast and then later went for a walk. As I watched the sunset over the ocean, savoring the spectacular beauty, I thought of God's description to Job of how He created everything. I realized that God is telling us something very profound every single day in this incredibly beautiful world that He has made for us if we will only open our eyes to the wonders around us. The light. The darkness. The sky, the ocean. Trees, vegetation, and flowers. Wildlife and birds. He is saying, "I am the Lord! Be still . . . and know that I am God." I've learned that stillness is more than just physically staying in one spot. It's possible to stay in one place and be stagnant. It's also possible to be very active yet be still in

one's spirit. Being still is going down deep to what's inside —
to the pain, the ambivalence of being human—and to ask
Jesus to enter there.

A lot of my healing came—body, soul, mind, and spirit—
as I began walking outside every day, just being present to
the beautiful surroundings and taking in the fact that God
made it; He made me; He loved me, and everything was
going to be all right. Being in nature is very healing—and
it's not just "nature"—it's God Himself saying, *I love you.
There is a plan. Trust Me.*

GOD RESTORED JOB AND GAVE HIM TWICE
AS MUCH AS HE'D HAD BEFORE—AFTER JOB
PRAYED FOR HIS FRIENDS

Job's three friends offered a sacrifice as God instructed
them to, then Job—again asserting his spiritual leadership—prayed for the three friends. There is something healing about getting one's mind off oneself; praying for others.
It is also remarkable that Job would pray for those who had
been judging him.

If anything is certain, it is that every one of life's trials, if only because it breaks the hard crust of our
physical and mental habits, creates, like the ploughing
of a field, an empty space where seed can be sown. In
the sudden void caused by a bereavement . . . an illness . . . failure . . . loneliness . . . your mind is assailed

by fundamental questions to which you hardly ever gave a thought in the coercive whirl of life.

—PAUL TOURNIER, *Creative Suffering*

CLAIM YOUR HEALING

The LORD will strengthen him on his bed of illness;
You will sustain him on his sickbed.
I said, "LORD, be merciful to me;
Heal my soul."

—PSALM 41:3–4

My dear friend suffers from multiple sclerosis. She has valiantly contended with the disease for several years— sometimes she's better and sometimes the disease causes her problems. She has resisted canes and walkers. Last year she went to a well-known healing evangelist for prayer and claimed her healing. But last Sunday she was in church in a wheelchair. In a way, I felt dismayed to see her in the wheelchair; and then I realized how glad I was to see her and gave her a big hug, wheelchair and all. I thought about her later as I left church to go home. There was something about embracing that wheelchair . . . It reminded me somehow of what it means to embrace the cross. I, too, have been praying for her healing. I, too, believe God heals. How, when, where, I don't know. It is a mystery how our sovereign God works. But maybe sometimes we need to "claim" our illness, claim our pain. I don't mean wallow in it or celebrate it. I just mean admit that it's there. Yes, seek healing through prayer. Seek practical medical answers. But pay attention to your pain and try to listen. What is it telling you about yourself? About your relationships with others, and your most important relationship, with God?

My husband is in almost constant pain with arthritis. He tries to do the right things and take certain medications, but I am amazed at how he puts a smile on his face and keeps going, which seems somehow to help lessen the pain.

Flora S. Wuellner wrote: "Our bodies—given to us as our lifelong companions, guides, and truth-tellers—are often the first to signal to us that we are carrying unfaced burdens of pain either from our personal lives or our communities. Learning to listen to our bodies is an essential spiritual discipline and an intrinsic part of healing prayer."[1]

Craig Barnes, in *Yearning: Living Between How It Is and How It Ought to Be,* wrote:

> Hope arises out of the hard truth of how things are. Christians will always live carrying in one hand the promise of how it will be and in the other the hard reality of how it is. To deny either is to hold only half of the gospel.
>
> What we find in the Scripture is the incredible promise that God has broken into our brokenness to

find us there. There is no promise that, having found us, He will paste our fractured lives back together.

This doesn't mean that all of life doesn't have to be brought under the healing of God. It does. But God's healing doesn't fit exactly with our yearnings to have the pain taken away. As a church member with cancer once told me, "There is a big difference between healing and avoiding death."

God's healing has more to do with learning to worship than it does with getting life fixed. What God is eager to heal are the sickness of the soul and the blindness of the heart that take us down a painful road away from His love. Worship is the means by which our eyes are opened.

In worshiping God we realize we were never created to be whole. God will not restore what we were never intended to have. What we were created to enjoy is fellowship with God, who alone is whole and complete.[2]

When we were publishing *Christian Parenting Today,* one of our readers told us her little girl sat in her lap and asked, "Mommy, is Jesus in your heart?" She said, "Yes, He certainly is." The little girl put her head up to her mommy's chest, listened, and said, "I hear Him!" Her mommy smiled and asked, "Well, what's He saying?" She listened again for a minute and then said, "I think He's making coffee!"

A friend of mine said to me, "These people who say they

hear from God—God said this and God said that. How do you hear from God, really?" Maybe we hear Him by inviting Him in where we are, in the midst of our pain—fellowship with Him—have "coffee" with Him! And as we spend time in His Word and with His people in the midst of the ordinary events of our lives, through our joys, and yes, through our pain, He reminds us that His grace is enough.

— REFLECTION —

Do you experience chronic physical pain? What "message" do you think your body is sending you? Is there an emotional pain that you are carrying? Consider asking for prayer for healing, and remember that He said, "I am the God that healeth thee."

— PRAYER —

Lord, I know You want us to know Your love—to know it down deep. Help us to truly receive Your grace by allowing You into those places of pain, the physical pain and the emotional pain deep inside where we are most weak and vulnerable; where we need Your healing touch. Give us the courage to open up and see the truth about ourselves. And then, Lord, to offer healing and grace to others by offering our presence and our prayers. In Christ's name. Amen.

4

~

THE DESERT OF EXHAUSTION

I cried to the LORD with my voice,
And He heard me from His holy hill.
I lay down and slept;
I awoke, for the LORD sustained me.

—Psalm 3:4–5

— SUGGESTED READING:
1 KINGS 18; 19; MARK 6:30–44 —

O ne night I wrote in my journal:

I am so tired . . . Constant meetings, company, and I suppose what makes me even more tired is the thought of what lies ahead. I can't hostess one more person, cook one more meal, wash one more load of clothes, answer one more phone call. I just want to be left alone. I can't stop giving, but I don't have anything left to give.

It's easy to see now, looking back, how I got to that place of exhaustion. My hands were full by being married to Bill, an entrepreneur who was publishing magazines (and I was helping him); parenting five growing, very active children—one with special needs; involvement in church, community, and volunteer prison work; along with writing and speaking deadlines. And the most convicting reason of all was that I rarely said, "No."

I was haunted by feeling there never was enough time to do all I needed to do. Never enough time. A friend gave me a framed saying: "God has given me a certain number of things to accomplish in my lifetime, and so far it looks as if I will never die."

But I hit the wall when it seemed my physical and emotional health broke. My exhaustion came from working too hard, not living a balanced life. I had been living with a diagnosis of systemic lupus erythematosus for four years, and just taking care of my family was a full-time job, not to mention all the other things I was trying to do, too—and do them well. Perhaps the driving force behind my getting to this place of exhaustion was the need to please everyone, to never confront. Most of the time I was in pain, fatigued, and overwhelmed.

A physician at the Mayo Clinic urged me to look at my depleted and exhausted life, reminding me that the cutting edge of medicine indicates that a majority of illnesses are caused by or exacerbated by the stress in our lives. A. Heschel said, "More people die in the epidemic of needs than in the epidemics of disease." I felt as if I were dying—something needed to change. On my flight home, I determined to take a hard look at my life.

ELIJAH'S STORY

And the angel of the LORD . . . touched him, and said, "Arise and eat, because the journey is too great for you."

—1 KINGS 19:7

After Elijah's great showdown and victory at Mount Carmel with the prophets of Baal, Jezebel was furious and promised to kill him. Suddenly this great, fearless prophet of God had a pressing need to get out of town. He ran for his life into the desert toward Mount Horeb.

Evidently he'd left in such a hurry that he hadn't brought any food or water with him, and at the end of running a whole day, he sat under a juniper tree, praying to die. He said, "It is enough! Now, LORD, take my life, for I am no better than my fathers!" (1 Kings 19:4). Exhausted, he fell asleep, and an angel touched him and said, "Arise and eat." Elijah looked, and there by his head was a cake baked on hot stones, and a jar of water. He ate and drank, and slept again. Once more the angel of the Lord awakened him after a time and encouraged him to eat and drink again because, the angel said, "The journey is too great for you." The food that God provided for him kept him going for forty days and nights as he journeyed to Mount Horeb (the same place Moses met God at the burning bush).

Often when we reach a desert place—especially if we are exhausted—we are in desperate need to be nourished, fed. The psalmist posed the question "Can God prepare a table in the wilderness?" (78:19). Well, He certainly can—and does. God provided the daily manna and the quail for the children of Israel. He fed them in the desert, gave them water. But how do we become nourished in our own desert experiences, especially when we are depleted by life?

As I began to take a hard look at my life, I realized that really, I had the kind of life I'd always wanted. But it was too much, and it was out of balance. God has made us with physical, spiritual, mental, and emotional needs. We are creatures of seasons and cycles and rhythms. Our very world dictates it: seasons, night and day. We need to sleep as well as be awake; play as well as work. We must be nourished in order to nourish others. We need rest.

When we don't respect our very real needs, we can find ourselves exhausted, wondering what went wrong. This often happens to driven people, and it's difficult for us to accept because suddenly it seems we lose our effectiveness, lose our ability to "do," the very thing we so highly prize. We go from high speed to zero. We crash.

You shall love the LORD your God with all your heart, with all your soul, with all your strength, and with all your mind.

—LUKE 10:27

OUR WHOLE PERSON—BODY, MIND, SOUL, AND SPIRIT—NEEDS REST

Hans Selye in *The Stress of Life* writes about how life is expendable—we literally spend our lives. And like a bank account, if we take continual withdrawals and do not make deposits, we become overdrawn. That was me. Over the years, I had not made the necessary "deposits"—I had been running in the red, emotionally and physically, for too long. I wasn't allowing for rest and relaxation. I wasn't allowing God to nourish me, even though I wanted my life to "feed" other people—my husband, my children, my church, my community, people who needed the Lord. The needs seemed so great, never-ending. And yet I missed a step— unless I received nourishment, there was no way I could continue to feed others.

Jesus said we are to love Him with our body, mind, soul, and spirit. That means loving Him with our whole selves, not just some splintered-off part. I heard someone say once that we are like houses with four rooms: body, soul, mind, and spirit; and that to be a truly balanced person, we must go into each of those rooms every day. When I got sick, I was loving God with my "mind" and my "spirit"; but I was neglecting loving Him with my physical self (strength) and with my soul (my emotions).

PHYSICAL REST

It is vain for you to rise up early,

To sit up late,

To eat the bread of sorrows;

For so He gives His beloved sleep.

— PSALM 127:2

I had been neglecting my physical self. If I had time to exercise, I would. Now I realized it was no longer an option; it was a necessity. The first thing I did was to start walking consistently. This continues to be one of my biggest stress-reducers. Just to get outside and see the sky lifts my spirits and seems to put life in perspective. I went to bed at night (this may seem like an elementary step, but before, if I had a deadline or more work to do, I would try to finish no matter how late, or early, the hour). I tried to make better food choices and began taking vitamins.

It was a lot of work dealing with all this, but I stubbornly persisted because I knew something had to change.

More than anything, I wanted to be an effective wife, mother, and friend. I realized I was carrying more than my share of the work around the house, albeit self-appointed, so I asked the family for more help. It also was helpful to adjust my expectations that everything need not be done to perfection, but to enjoy life, mess and all.

When I'm under mental and spiritual stress, I find it helps bring balance to do something physical: working in the yard, baking, or playing the piano. Trying to do a craft would, quite frankly, drive me crazy. My husband, however, finds it refreshing to make something with his hands, or craft something in his workshop. Different people find different ways of bringing balance to their physical lives. Thomas à Kempis wrote these words of wisdom centuries ago: "So long as you wear this mortal body, you will be subject to weariness and sadness of heart . . . When this happens, you will be wise to resort to humble, exterior tasks, and to restore yourself by good works."[1]

MENTAL REST

Zeal for Your house has eaten me up.

—PSALM 69:9

I took a stress management class, and one of the first and most important principles I learned was: Although there are some circumstances that are not possible to change, I can change the way I "frame" or see them. This simple insight opened my thinking and continues to help me. In other words, I focus on what I can do rather than on what I can't do. See the possibility, not the obstacle. This simple insight helps me because I often tend to see the problem rather than the solution. This is partly why I was feeling overwhelmed by loss—I was seeing the fear rather than the opportunity.

I quit carrying my briefcase with me everywhere I went. For years, I never went on vacation, even overnight, without taking some work with me, a manuscript to read, or a book to work on. Even in my reading I tried to bring some balance and began to read some fiction and renewed my love of poetry, balancing out the theological and deeper spiritual reading. I like the mental stimulation of challenging ideas, but I realized I had forgotten about poetry. Poetry is a different kind of reading that is like an oasis— I've made it a point to carry a small book of poetry with me when I travel to read a few lines and memorize them for the sheer pleasure of the words.

In our world with everything coming at us full speed, we must have boundaries or we can become overtaken. There are times to turn off the TV; stay home instead of spending mindless hours shopping; or let the phone machine answer the calls and return them later. Perhaps the secret of a successful life is skillful editing. As I prayerfully try to decide what to write in this book and what not to write, I must edit out many pages so that the message comes through, is not obscured. And so it is in life—we must say no to some things in order to say a burning yes to the right things.

SOUL REST

In the words of Walter Brueggemann, the question many of us ask these days is: "Is there a word from the Lord that will let me live? . . . Is there a word that will rescue me from my exhausted coping?"[2]

At the time I was going through a personal evaluation, our magazine was going through a redesign—something periodicals do occasionally to stay fresh. The consultant who critiqued the magazine commented, "Your magazine is good, but it's overdesigned. You have too much text and too much illustration. The text and illustrations are good, but you need more white space to set off what you want to say."

A light went on inside me: White space! That's what I needed. My life was overdesigned—full of good things, but so full that it was empty. True to my personality, I craved spontaneity, but I did not have any of that. There was no time for it because there was too much to do, and not enough time to do it. Perhaps if I had been living with such a crammed-full life only a year or so, I wouldn't have crashed as I did—but I had gone this way for several years. I rarely cut myself "slack." In order to get everything done, I had to do several things at once—fold clothes while talking on the phone, work in the car, read manuscripts in waiting rooms. Every minute had to count for me.

"Soul rest" means taking time to acknowledge honest, real emotions, and then letting them go. I had not taken time for this, and as a consequence I believe I was suffering physically. I hadn't taken time to grieve the loss of my father. I just didn't have time to feel, although I was consumed by worry and anxiety, bordering on being neurotic.

One day on my way home I got stuck for fifteen minutes in a construction line, and I was absolutely fuming. I had a house to clean, correspondence to deal with, phone calls to make, dental appointments to make for the children, shopping and menu lists to complete, I needed to prepare for an editorial planning meeting—I did not have time for this!

I finally turned the car off and leaned back and opened the sunroof. The thought *What . . . a . . . gorgeous . . . day!* finally filtered in. Warm sunshine and the musky smell of pine needles filled the air. The sky was blue as it only can be in central Oregon in a blaze of glory. I looked up and saw a black hawk circling high, soaring effortlessly on the air currents. A vaguely familiar quote having to do with "birds of the air" and "will He not care much more for you" made itself at home in my mind.

Why can't I be like that bird—just be? Just enjoy God's creation? Why can't I?

It was not so much the physical work that was smothering me (although it was considerable), but the worry and anxiety that I internalized were taking their toll. I worried over our learning-disabled daughter, Amy (How could I help her?); I worried over our four sons (Would they make good choices?); I worried about my husband's weight (Would he stay healthy?).

I had to realize it was good to be concerned and to pray, but I needed to "resign from running the universe" —to let go of trying to control. Soul rest means coming to Jesus with all our anxieties, fears, and worries and trusting Him with them. It is a conscious decision: "Commit [which literally means to 'roll off onto'] your way to the LORD, trust also in Him, and He shall bring it to pass" (Ps. 37:5).

SPIRITUAL REST

Come to Me, all you who labor and are heavy laden, and I will give you rest. Take My yoke upon you and learn from Me, for I am gentle and lowly in heart, and you will find rest for your souls.

—MATTHEW 11:28–29

I learned that it's important to be spiritually balanced, too. Years ago a neighbor commented to me somewhat wistfully, "You're always dressed up and you're always going to church." I cringe as I remember that because I didn't have time for her—time to just talk and be her friend. I was too busy "doing" spirituality.

Let's face it, we religious types can be obnoxious. Dr. M. Scott Peck relates that years ago he was involved with a team of people, and one of them, a Christian woman, seemed unable to speak more than two sentences without using the name of Jesus. It was bothering some of the others on the team. The woman saw Dr. Peck as a mentor, and she came to him, asking why she seemed to be alienating people. He told her frankly that he believed the other members of the team were feeling preached to—that they wanted her as a teammate, not a preacher. She asked in amazement what she should do. Dr. Peck encouraged her not to give up a shred of her faith, but instead, to try a discipline with the group. He said, "I've heard tell of certain Christian monks and nuns who upon occasion practice a strange kind of spiritual discipline. They take a vow—just as they would a vow of poverty or chastity or obedience— to not speak the name of Jesus out loud for a year. They remain free to use his name in their hearts and prayer, but they renounce their need to speak it publicly. As I said, it's a strange kind of discipline, but I wonder if it wouldn't be a useful one for you at this particular point."

To Dr. Peck's amazement, the woman followed his advice and rapidly became one of the most successful and constructive team members. Later she told him, "It's bizarre . . . Jesus has become ever more important to me over the past year." Dr. Peck went on to say that the woman eventually became his spiritual mentor.[3]

I swallowed my pride and decided to talk to a counselor who could give me insight and perspective I wouldn't get anywhere else. I wanted to know, *Why do I drive myself so?*

This was a huge step for me because it confronted my pride. In retrospect, it was a valuable investment because I took time to honestly understand what was driving me. I learned that early impressions are powerful. I grew up singing about grace, but I didn't live it—works and performance were the way to acceptance. I needed to truly "learn" of Jesus, learn of His grace.

Everything I did came back at me with an accusation: *You've neglected nutrition, dental follow-up for the kids, eye exams, helping the children learn to read better. You need to clean closets. The refrigerator is awful. You could have written that article better. You've neglected your own body, exercise, diet. You're way behind on your correspondence; now they will suspect what is only true—you're unreliable and incompetent.* And so on and on the subtle but constant condemnation went in the grooves of my brain, reminding me that much was hanging on my shoulders and I was not keeping up.

And if this was the kind of Christ I wanted to give and communicate to others, it certainly wasn't the real Jesus. Who would want my kind of religion? Our Lord is not a harsh taskmaster; He is not judgmental or condemning. Instead He is "a God full of compassion, and gracious, long-suffering and abundant in mercy and truth" (Ps. 86:15).

GRACE IN THE DESERT

I am convinced a major reason I found myself in the desert ultimately was spiritual—from a twisted view of God that He was a remote deity and I had to work constantly to try to gain His approval. "Do more, pray more, do it better" was not God's voice.

These can be difficult voices to contend with because it seems they push us to do good things, Christian sorts of things. How can good things be bad? To counteract these thoughts, I began memorizing verses about grace, often seeing them for the first time. By grace am I saved through faith—not of works, lest I boast. Grace means not of myself. It is God's gift. Gift. No strings. Accepted into the Beloved, just as I am.

Doing good things with excellence is a good quality and should be rewarded, but it's impossible to reach perfection. It is astounding to think how we can be wounded by life and then adopt those very wounds as our way of living.

I wrote this prayer in my journal:

> *God, how I need a fresh baptism of Your love and grace. I cannot do one more thing without You. I cannot love in my self. Help me put away childish things. I do not want to be a little girl achieving and performing to be noticed. By grace I am saved. Help me to look into my children's eyes, their faces, and let them know I love them—not for what they do, but for who they are.*

Unfortunately, in seeing ourselves as we truly are, not all that we see is beautiful and attractive. This is undoubtedly why we flee silence. We do not want to be

confronted with our own hypocrisy, our phoniness. We
see how false and fragile is the false self we project. We
have to go through this painful experience to come to
our true self. It is a harrowing journey, a death to self—
the false self—and no one wants to die. But it is the
path to life, to freedom, to peace, to true love. And it
begins with silence. We cannot give ourselves in love if
we do not know and possess ourselves. This is the great
value of silence. It is the pathway to all we truly want.

—M. BASIL PENNINGTON, *A Place Apart* [4]

It is not easy for some of us to think in fresh patterns, to
frame our thoughts in positive ways . . . to live in grace. We
can get in habits and patterns of thinking, and some of us
need to *contend* for grace, which the writer of Hebrews
described as being "diligent to enter that rest" (4:11). I am
grateful that Bill supported my receiving counseling and
efforts to honestly confront my life. It is a great gift to allow
our spouses and children to grow—to affirm them instead of
being threatened by growth.

Often people who are determined to break out of their
cocoon to become "themselves" are convinced by current
thought that a complete change of life and work or a divorce
is often a rite of passage, a way to grow. But I have come to
believe that we can grow stronger and deeper within our
important covenants in ways we would not think possible if
we have the courage and tenacity to persist.

I've enjoyed watching our children go through their stages: the terrible twos, the enchanting preschool years, the junior high jitters, the magnificent high school years. I can reassure other parents who are tearing their hair out, this, too, will pass—it's a phase. But just because a child reaches the magic age of twenty-one does not mean he or she will stop going through phases. We should not want them to. Growth demands seasons—seasons of the desert as well as the oasis.

Jesus went about doing good—dealing with what came His way. Of course He prepared first by being a son; being in a carpenter's shop; going through baptism; going through the wilderness experience. And then He began His ministry. It's important to recognize the sequence of life . . . passages. Seasons.

One recent early morning I watched the sun come up over the trees and shine on the freshly fallen snow. How achingly beautiful it was, I thought, a new day, new mercies. And before I jumped into the day, I allowed myself to be nourished by the Word. I have found that it is the Word that sustains me, renews me. I grew up studying the Bible, reading it, using its truths to teach, to write, to admonish. But I learned in the desert experience to read it for my food, my daily manna.

That morning I read Micah 6:6–8: "With what shall I come before the LORD . . . ? Shall I come before Him with burnt offerings . . . thousands of rams . . . ten thousand rivers of oil . . . my firstborn? He has shown you . . . what is good; and what does the LORD require of you but to do justly, to love mercy, and to walk humbly with your God?" What simple, profound wisdom.

I believe that when God takes us to new places, His Word will come alive in a fresh way to us there. Jeremiah 15:16 says this so eloquently: "Your words were found, and I ate them, and Your word was to me the joy and rejoicing of my heart; for I am called by Your name, O LORD God of hosts." In other words, take the time to nourish yourself, to reflect on the beautiful, complex gift of your life, and to be still and know God.

Perhaps in this desert of exhaustion you realize that you have not grieved some of your losses, that you have denied some powerful emotions. Perhaps you will see that you have neglected and abused your physical condition. Perhaps you are not respecting your intellect; you are not being challenged enough there, or you are out of balance in your thinking. And most important, perhaps you have internalized some faulty spiritual beliefs that have taken you down a dead-end road.

Allow yourself to be replenished and nourished by His Word. Hear and take in His message: "Look at the birds of the air . . . your heavenly Father feeds them. Are you not of more value than they?" (Matt. 6:26).

Sabbath "Rest" Brings Restoration

A lot of the early American pioneers going west on their epic journey observed a Sabbath, a holy day of rest. There were some wagon trains that didn't, as they believed they needed to hurry to get over the mountains before the cold weather began. But there were many who did vote to keep the Sabbath. They believed they needed it for the journey; needed it to pace themselves; and their animals and children needed it as well. Sometimes we think we don't have time to stop and rest, and yet what wisdom there is in it.

These days I believe we need to revisit the concept of keeping the Sabbath holy. I'm not talking about a rigid legalistic observance, but the concept of taking time off to pace ourselves for our journey and to replenish ourselves. As the angel told Elijah, "Arise and eat; the journey is too great for you."

The pioneers needed the Sabbath to help them keep going. Even if there were days they needed to travel for a little while on the Sabbath, they just went as far as they needed for water, or for good grazing and then stopped. One of the pioneer women wrote in her diary: "Sabbath eve: Did not go forward today . . . everyone anxious to go ahead and we amongst them but to rest a day will do our cattle a great deal of good and we think will do us no harm."[5] The Eighty-fourth Psalm says that He provides us springs and places of rest in the desert—oases—if we will stop, find them, and be replenished.

Sometimes we must stop in order to go forward. We need the Sabbath to rest, to find our "center" in God again. One pioneer woman who seemed overcome by the vastness of the land wrote in her diary on the journey west to Oregon: "I write in order to remember who I am." Sometimes it seems like a vast desert around us, and journaling, being still, finding a place of quiet reflection and honesty to pray are good ways to "remember who we are."[6]

An Observance of the Heart

"There remains therefore," Hebrews 4:9 says, "a rest for the people of God." In the thought-provoking and convicting book of Hebrews—especially chapters 3 and 4—we are urged to make every effort to enter into rest, into belief. Why did God rest on the seventh day? Because His works were finished and He stopped to savor the fact that it was done, that it was good.

Certain holidays—"holy days"—help remind us of the real thing. Anniversaries remind us of commitments we've made. Birthdays help us celebrate the person, commemorate a milestone. And so it is with the "Sabbath" concept—it is an observance of the heart. Keeping the Sabbath in our hearts can help us remember, "It is finished." We can simply rest in His grace and provision for our lives and "enter into rest," accepting the work He has done.

When we reach a place of burnout, sometimes we are tempted to quit everything, or to radically change our location or vocation. Yet if we look at Elijah, we see that first God replenished and nourished him in the wilderness before he went on to Mount Horeb. It took him a while to hear the still, small voice, but when he did, he responded. His next step was to go back and invest in others' ministry, to keep developing the message.

The next step after you've been fed and replenished can be your most productive time. But it takes prayer, thinking, discerning. It takes listening for the still, small voice. How we need "Sabbath" to remember our High Priest who completed the work, to savor the concept of grace. To remember that we are not driven; we are led by One who has finished the work of redemption. To remember that Jesus does not drive His sheep; He leads us beside still waters . . . He restores our souls.

Jesus was in a deserted place, but lots of people—multitudes—had followed Him there, hungry to hear His words. Jesus had compassion on them because they were like sheep without a shepherd, and how they needed to hear. But after a while Jesus' disciples came to Him, concerned, and said, "This is a deserted place, and already the hour is late. Send them away, that they may go into the surrounding country and villages and buy themselves bread; for they have nothing to eat." And that's when the miracle happened. One young boy had thought ahead and brought his lunch: five barley loaves and two fish (see Mark 6:30–44). As a mother of four sons, I know that growing boys give a lot of thought to the next meal! The boy generously offered his lunch—such as it was—and at Jesus' blessing, it fed a multitude—with twelve baskets left over.

You may be saying, "How can my messed-up life feed anybody?" When we let God into our desert places, become nourished by Him there, and then give out of restoration, it's powerful giving. And at His touch, it becomes miraculous—enough to feed the hungry.

— REFLECTION —

When it comes right down to it—you are the gatekeeper, the steward of your life. Are you taking time to be replenished for your journey ahead? Which of the four areas of your life (body, mind, soul, and spirit) most need replenishing? What steps can you take to do that?

— PRAYER —

Fill my cup, Lord. Father, I am on my face before You. I cannot go one more step without You, without knowing You are with me. Lead me beside still waters. Restore my soul. Renew my mind. Show me how to dream my dreams with and for You. Remind me that my audience is You, only You. Teach me to love You with my body, soul, mind, and spirit. Amen.

5

~

THE DESERT OF CIRCUMSTANCES

I am like a city under siege.

—Job 19:6 NLT

— SUGGESTED READING: GENESIS 37; 39–50 —

TIME AND CHANCE HAPPEN TO ALL

Have you noticed there are just some days when everything goes wrong? The dryer quits; the dishwasher overflows; your children have the flu. Frustrating! Or to make things worse, a whole lot of big things go wrong in a year. Your job ends, your church has problems, your best friends divorce, your son goes into a major rebellion, and on and on. Things pile up, and where once you had it pretty much together and were cruising through life, suddenly it's turned into a desert around you.

I've had days—and years—like that. And even though we know that's life, sometimes we can't help asking, "Why?" There are probably many reasons and maybe some we'll never know. Ecclesiastes 9:11 says, "The race is not to the swift, nor the battle to the strong, nor bread to the wise, nor riches to men of understanding, nor favor to men of skill; but time and chance happen to them all."

We don't necessarily get what we deserve. Losses happen. Death separates loved ones. Illness may strike. There are no perfect children, no perfect marriages.

I've spent most of my life trying to be a good wife, mother, friend, follower of Christ. But it doesn't really matter how "good" we are or how hard we try. Circumstances don't stop simply because we reach a certain place in life. But I am learning that it's essential to be obedient to God, regardless.

OBEDIENCE . . . REGARDLESS

Even though we can't understand why things are happening (and maybe we never will), we can cling to God with all we have within the situation. Job had no clue why all the terrible things were happening to him as he wasn't in on the conversation between God and Satan about what was to be unleashed on him. Job's friends had a lot of answers for him (Job had to have sinned for these calamities to have happened). But Job stubbornly hung on to the character and nature of God, and although he honestly grieved and expressed his pain, he knew what he knew.

Life can take it out of you—changes; people you once were intimately involved with now absent; the loss of dreams and plans. There are times we can literally feel beat up by life. Both of my parents suffered extreme hardship and suffering early on in their lives—they lost their parents; they lost their homes; their lives were deeply impacted by the Great Depression, as many were in this nation. When they came to Christ as young adults, their lives did not suddenly become problem-free; what they did have, however, were joy and purpose and a compass, real Christian community, and an opportunity for fulfillment.

How do we respond when we get slammed in the desert of circumstances? It's an opportunity to respond with fear or with faith. In the desert of negative circumstances sometimes it's hard to have perspective, to respond in a positive way. We are tempted to complain, like the children of Israel. Why no water? Why the same old manna, day after day? Why is everybody against us?

Perhaps the lesson here is that when we are in one of life's deserts—for whatever the reason—it can be overwhelming to look around us. The land is too big. We're too lost. So God says, "Every day, I will send manna. For that day only!" It is a lesson of trust, of obedience. One day at a time is all God asks of us while we are in the desert. Strength for one day's journey is enough.

Fear not, for I have redeemed you;

I have called you by your name;

You are Mine.

When you pass through the waters, I will be with you;

And through the rivers, they shall not overflow you.

When you walk through the fire, you shall not

   be burned,

Nor shall the flame scorch you.

For I am the LORD your God.

—ISAIAH 43:1–3

LESSONS FROM JOSEPH

Joseph, the blessed and wanted son of Rachel, Jacob's beloved wife, had some very unfair things happen to him as his life began to unfold. First, his mother died giving birth to his little brother, Benjamin.

Still, Joseph was uniquely gifted by God to discern dreams. Perhaps there was something about Joseph that reminded his father, Jacob, of Rachel, whom he'd dearly loved. At any rate, Jacob made Joseph a specially embroidered coat of many colors, and Genesis 37:3 says that Jacob "loved Joseph more than all his children." His older brothers were jealous of Joseph's gifts and their father's obvious favoritism toward their younger brother, and they began plotting how to get rid of him. One day when Joseph went out to the fields to check on his brothers, they grabbed him and threw him in a pit. Later, when a band of Midianites came by on their way to Egypt, they sold their brother into slavery. Reuben, the oldest brother, who wasn't around at the time, had intended to come back and rescue Joseph, but when he got back, it was too late. The deed was done and Joseph was gone—never to be seen again, the brothers thought. Scripture says that Joseph, probably about seventeen years of age at the time, had begged and pleaded with his brothers not to sell him.

What a heart-rending scene it must have been as this sensitive, gifted young man was sold by his own brothers into Egypt as a slave. How unjust, and what a betrayal. The brothers' jealousy and hatred were so great they even overshadowed what their cruel action toward Joseph would do to their father, Jacob. They dipped Joseph's coat of many colors into goat's blood and showed it to their father, telling him they'd found it and wild animals must have killed Joseph. Jacob's grief was great, and he refused to be comforted, saying he would die mourning his son (see Gen. 37).

But God wasn't finished with Joseph. He ended up being purchased by Potiphar, a captain of the guard in Pharaoh's army. Again, Joseph's talent and gracious personality helped him rise to the top. And he was betrayed by Potiphar's wife, who tried to seduce him. Angry at his rebuff, she pulled off his coat as he fled the room to get away from her. She showed the garment to her husband, claiming Joseph had tried to rape her. (What is there about Joseph and his coats? His coat of many colors was given to his father as proof that he'd been killed by some wild animal; his garment in Potiphar's house was shown as proof of his aggression toward Potiphar's wife. Maybe the lesson here is that what you see may not be the whole story!)

Joseph was thrown into prison. Again, Joseph stayed true no matter what—used his gifts no matter what—and the keeper of the prison eventually put Joseph in charge of all the other prisoners. Two of his prison-mates, Pharaoh's chief butler and his chief baker, each had troublesome dreams, which Joseph accurately interpreted. The baker was executed, and the butler was restored to his position in Pharaoh's house. Joseph asked the butler to remember him to Pharaoh, but the butler forgot . . . until two years later when Pharaoh had a troublesome dream that no one could interpret. However, all this time Joseph continued to use his gifts, continued to keep his attitude right in his administrative position in the prison. As Pharaoh puzzled over the meaning of his dreams, the butler finally remembered Joseph. How often do we have good intentions only to not follow through?

Pharaoh sent for Joseph, who gave him an accurate interpretation of the dream, which had to do with an approaching famine. Pharaoh was so impressed by Joseph and his plan to safeguard against the famine that he pardoned him and put him to work immediately to take measures to protect the nation. Joseph soon rose through the ranks. As the years went by, he became a powerful man in Egypt, second only to Pharaoh. Pharaoh said to Joseph, "Inasmuch as God has shown you all this, there is no one as discerning and wise as you" (Gen. 41:39).

How did Joseph end up on top? The circumstances of his life were unfair, but Joseph's resilience began years before, when he learned what was right and wrong from his father. It continued in the house of Potiphar, where he did the right thing, regardless. It continued in the prison, where he did the right thing and kept using his gifts and talents right where he was, even in terrible circumstances. God restored and blessed Joseph.

Then came the difficult time that was predicted. Famine hit the region hard, affecting not only Egypt but also Joseph's homeland—and his father and his brothers. The brothers heard there was grain to buy in Egypt, so they journeyed there. You can imagine Joseph's amazement to recognize his brothers as they came calling. It's interesting to see how Joseph played a few head games with them, testing them.

It's ironic that Joseph's gift of interpreting dreams—the very thing his brothers had ridiculed and hated him for—became the means of their having grain to keep them from famine. And the irony of it was that Joseph was there to give it to them, thus redeeming their entire family from starvation.

Jesus didn't promise to change the circumstances around us, but he did promise great peace and pure joy to those who would learn to believe that God actually controls all things.

—MERLIN R. CAROTHERS[1]

WHAT CAN WE LEARN FROM JOSEPH'S EXAMPLE?

Circumstances most painful to bear can come at the hands of our own "brothers." Often family members do not see each other as unique, gifted people with potential. We "pigeonhole" our brothers and sisters. We can be jealous of their gifts and qualities. How subtle yet how effective are put-downs from family members. A mere look; an expression; only two or three words from a family member can be all it takes for some of us to hit a tailspin; we willingly shape our lives to fit their expectations instead of truly following God, from whom we are. Joseph did not deny who he was in order to please others, and ultimately, he succeeded.

We must keep using our gifts for good regardless of where we are. Joseph kept using his intellect, his administrative skills, and his gift of discernment no matter where he was—in slavery; in Potiphar's house; even in prison; and in Pharaoh's court. The very quality of Joseph's that his brothers hated became the quality that saved them and the rest of the family. He kept a right spirit, a good attitude. Joseph's negative circumstances didn't last forever. He got out of prison. Time passed. Things changed. The famine ended. But the catalyst of Joseph consistently responding in a positive way— regardless of circumstances—was the quality that carried him through to success and triumph.

We, too, can keep focused on the Big Picture. Although it was impossible for Joseph to know as he was carried off by the Midianites that someday he would see his family again, someday his life would have purpose and meaning, someday he would have his own loving family, he didn't seem to waste time agonizing over the "whys" of the situation. Instead he focused on keeping his own attitude right, and on what he could do where he was. And finally he saw his circumstances change. His comment to his astonished brothers when they realized who he was: "Do not therefore be grieved or angry with yourselves because you sold me here; for God sent me before you to preserve life" (Gen. 45:5). Joseph had an unshakable belief that God was going to work all things for good.

We, too, can believe that in our circumstances, a sovereign God is in control, and we should not waste energy blaming others. The burden of response is not tied to the circumstances, dire though they may be. It is our response *in* the circumstances. What will be our attitude, our spirit? Whom do we believe? That is the true test.

We must forgive those who have hurt us. Joseph didn't deny his grief, his anger, or his love for his family. Scripture records that he was so overcome with emotion that he had to go to a room at times to weep openly. And yet Joseph forgave his brothers for the betrayal and even fed them. He didn't try to get revenge or punish his brothers. He cared for them; even provided a permanent place for the whole tribe to live—sixty-six people!

There is something healing about giving out of our pain, our hurt. Holding on to a grudge only magnifies it and hurts ourselves more than anything. Joseph's personal desert of circumstances prepared him to provide for others who would face their own actual famine. Maybe the lesson here is that no sorrow, no difficulty—regardless how unfair, how random—is wasted when we believe in the Redeemer and do the right thing, regardless.

Our desert of circumstances—if given wholly to Him—can provide bread in the wilderness for others—yes, even for our own selves.

> And we know that all things work together for good to those who love God, to those who are the called according to His purpose.
>
> —ROMANS 8:28

THE DESERT: A PLACE OF PURPOSE

I recently discovered that the old Santiam Wagon Trail runs right by our house. Its unmistakable swath still cuts through the giant ponderosa pines as it winds its way west toward Santiam Pass and the Willamette Valley, some of the trail now overgrown by smaller trees and interrupted by logging roads.

It's amazing to think that little more than a hundred years ago, wagons were tediously pushing their way through here on their way to the fertile Willamette Valley. One of the most difficult places of the journey was when they finally reached the Oregon Territories and discovered that the eastern side was largely desert. By that time their food was running low, water was scarce, and their animals were worn out. I am struck by the strength and persistence of the pioneers as they endured incredible hardship: death of many of their family members, starvation, poor water, accidents, birth along the way in the most inconvenient places and times. Life didn't stop just because they were crossing the desert.

Their journey west was painstakingly slow as they often carved out new roads, averaging about ten miles a day—a one-way trip to our local school. Some couldn't stand the rigors of the trail and went back to their old life. But in reading the diaries of those who pushed on regardless of the hardships, many knew they were part of a journey of biblical proportions that was difficult but exhilarating. As someone said, "Some goals are so worthy, it's glorious even to fail."

I walked through the old path, looking at the faintly worn tracks with new appreciation. *What's left to pioneer,* I wondered. *What worlds are left to conquer?* Perhaps the greatest, most challenging adventures of all await us in the realm of the spirit, as we learn to respond with faithfulness and integrity in spite of the most difficult and perplexing circumstances imaginable.

One afternoon as I finished speaking at a retreat, a woman came to me, her eyes brimming with tears. She said, "God promises that He will not give us more than we can bear. Yet I am about to tell Him He has gone over the line with me!" She went on to describe the circumstances of her life: her children on drugs, in rebellion. But the final straw was that she had just discovered that her husband, a pastor, was addicted to pornography.

What do we say to someone in her situation? I encouraged her to keep trusting God, even though she doesn't understand. I encouraged her to believe in Him, and to believe for the future—not because of circumstances, but in spite of them, and because of the unfailing nature of God. Luke 1:45 said this about Mary, Jesus' mother: "Blessed is she who believed, for there will be a fulfillment of those things which were told her from the Lord." If Mary had looked at the circumstances at the cross, surely her heart would have failed. But after the Cross, there was a resurrection. After the Resurrection, there was a pentecost.

It's in the difficult, in-between places where Jesus asks, "Will you drink the cup with Me?" The hard sayings of Jesus touch the core of our hearts and we cannot be neutral about them. Do we love Him, regardless of our circumstances? Are we willing to trust Him, no matter what?

HE REDEEMS ALL THAT
WE PLACE IN HIS HAND

For the first time in my life I saw the truth as it is set into song by so many poets, proclaimed as the final wisdom by so many thinkers. The truth—that love is the ultimate and highest goal to which man can aspire. Then I grasped the meaning of the greatest secret that human poetry and human thought and belief have to impart: The salvation of man is through love and in love. For the first time in my life I was able to understand the meaning of the words, "the angels are lost in perpetual adoration of an infinite glory."

—VIKTOR FRANKL, NAZI DEATH CAMP SURVIVOR,
Man's Search for Meaning[2]

———————————————◦———————————————

There are times when life is too much and we may feel like giving up. But that's when we must remember our greatest example, Jesus Christ, and "consider Him . . . lest you become weary and discouraged in your souls" (Heb. 12:3). Each of us has a unique and miraculous life—a wonderful gift from God, and it's important to see what exactly is in that gift, and how God is refining us and making us vessels of honor.

It is important to discern our times. The early pioneers had to discern, to understand what they were in for on their rigorous journey through the wilderness. It was rough. It is estimated that one out of ten people died and at least thirty-four thousand people died along the way. The circumstances of their journey were terrible—the cholera, the disease, the accidents, little children falling out of the back of the wagons, women dying in childbirth.

They had to understand what they were in for so they could take the right things on their journey. What are our times? Ecclesiastes 8:5–6 says this: "A wise man's heart discerns both time and judgment, because for every matter there is a time and judgment." You and I need to discern our times so that we have the "right stuff" to keep us going through hard circumstances.

WHAT ARE OUR TIMES?

IT IS A LAWLESS TIME

Judges 21:25 says everyone did what was right in his own eyes. People can justify anything if they get the right lawyers (and we see this all the time in the news and stories we hear). It's not so much a matter now of what is right; rather, it's who will prevail? It's frightening to see in our own culture that when the law is no longer written on our hearts—and we cannot assume that the Judeo-Christian ethic will be respected anymore—there is no bottom line. Anarchy and chaos can happen because the heart is desperately wicked, and we will go our own way without God's laws. Right has become wrong and wrong has become right. It's all turned upside down.

As we look around us, there is much injustice. Injustice can be very difficult to live with. There are many things that are just not fair. To counteract this, we must know God's laws— what's right and what's wrong, to write them on our hearts and teach them to our children and then to live by them.

It is also a biblically ignorant time. It used to be that a lot of people were raised in Sunday school and church and had a basic knowledge of the Bible, but that is not necessarily so these days.

IT IS AN ACCELERATED TIME

Our lives are not simple; we have many choices and options. A survey was done not long ago to ask why so many Americans feel under pressure, behind the curve all the time, with a to-do list that doesn't get checked off. People believed that as a whole, we are working more hours than we used to. But we're not! We're actually working less. What has increased is our sense of what is necessary in our lives. (For instance, we not only need a phone, we need e-mail, the cell phone, the fax, etc.) A medical expert commented that "civilization's three major killers are not heart disease, cancer, and accidents, but telephones, calendars, and clocks."

BUT THE GOOD NEWS IS,
IT ALSO IS A SPIRITUALLY HUNGRY TIME

There's a great vacuum in all of us that only God can fill, and it is a tremendous opportunity for us, the church. It's a time to know what captures our own hearts and have a fresh understanding of God as we read the Bible and trust Him.

THE MORE SOME THINGS CHANGE,
THE MORE THEY STAY THE SAME

What did these people bring, our predecessors who came west, these pioneers, the people who settled this part of the country? What did they bring? Not much. They brought their families, a few animals, and hoped they all would make it, but not everybody did. Essentially they brought themselves: their hopes, who they were as people, their heritage, and their dreams. And that is what we have.

That is what you bring on your journey—yourself. Our circumstances are all so different, although we have the same universal needs to be loved; to have a purpose; to belong. There are times you go through enormous trials and losses and sometimes people cannot understand your grace, your calm. God gives us grace for the moment, when we need it.

Jesus said in Matthew 11:28: "Come to Me, all you who labor and are heavy laden, and I will give you rest." Come into the secret place . . . the desert can be a secret place with Him . . . just come. Be there with simplicity, coming into His presence, letting Him minister to you where you are without waiting to get everything together.

THE LOVE OF GRANDPARENTS

In the past few years, we have entered the ranks of grandparenthood and have two grandchildren: Will, three; and Kendsy, one year. There is something so renewing and refreshing about little children. We kept them last week for a few days while their parents were out of town, and after they went home, I thought, *Neither of those two little charmers has read a book on how to get their needs met, nor taken a course on it, but they certainly know how.*

We can make getting our needs met by God unnecessarily complicated. I love to see Kendsy hold her arms up to be held. She's a tiny little miss, and when those arms go straight up, she is irresistible. Our Lord says, "Except you become as little children, you cannot enter the kingdom." He invites, "Come unto Me . . ." Children run into their parents' arms, knowing they can trust them to get their needs met, knowing that their presence is enough for any need they may have. I think He is saying that to us, His children: "Come into My presence, just as you are, and somehow everything will be all right."

My grandmother Olson had more than her share of negative circumstances. She married John, a man ten years older than she. He was talented and funny, but after only eight years of marriage and four small children, it became apparent that he was mentally ill. My grandfather had to be institutionalized, as in those days they had no effective treatment for his illness. My grandmother was then on her own with four children during the Depression, trying to survive.

Her circumstances were unbelievably difficult. Her oldest daughter died at age twenty-three, leaving three small children under three years of age. My grandmother tried to help her son-in-law and small grandchildren the best she could, but she still had children of her own to feed and care for as well. The son-in-law remarried and moved several times. How my grandmother loved those children—especially her first granddaughter, Clarice—and how she agonized over them.

Later, after all the children were grown, my grandmother met Jesus and her life was brand-new. Times got better for her; yet I remember my grandmother praying daily for her daughter's children, especially for her first granddaughter, Clarice. My grandmother died twenty-three years ago, not knowing where the grandchildren were as she had lost track of the family.

THE LOST IS FOUND

Last fall I spoke to a women's group in Alaska, and an attractive young woman with a slightly familiar look walked into the conference room. I discovered she was Clarice's daughter! Clarice was now ill in a nursing home, but as my long-lost cousin began to fill in the blanks of what had happened to Clarice, I realized I was looking at the beautiful result of my grandmother's prayers. After Clarice's tempestuous early life, she had moved to Alaska, become a Christian, married a wonderful man, and had three great children.

My grandmother died not knowing what had happened to her grandchildren . . . and yet she knew the character of God. She knew that she could trust Him with her dearest prayers. I am now a grandmother. I understand the love, the prayers, the heart that is given so freely to our children and grandchildren, the longing that all shall be well with them.

As I follow in the faith of my mother and my grandmothers, I wonder who will be following my footsteps. I pray that they will see a walk of obedience regardless of the circumstances, knowing someday all will be understood. And until then, we can hold to His hand, knowing He knows the way through.

— REFLECTION —

Read Joseph's amazing story in Genesis 37, 39–50. Do you identify with any of Joseph's circumstances? What can you learn from his life that will apply to your own situation?

— PRAYER —

My Father—Rock of my salvation, when I think I am walking in the light of understanding, help me to be sure the Light is You. When I am walking in darkness, on shifting ground, remind me that You are still leading me by the hand . . . no matter that I cannot feel Your touch. Remind me when I am passing through even the driest place that You are ahead of me, opening secret springs of water for my soul. Amen.

—JOHN OF THE CROSS, *You Set My Spirit Free*,
PARAPHRASED BY DAVID HAZARD[3]

6

~

THE DESERT Of WANDERING

And you shall remember that the LORD your God led
you all the way these forty years in the wilderness, to
humble you and test you, to know what was in your
heart, whether you would keep His commandments or
not. So He humbled you, allowed you to hunger, and
fed you with manna which you did not know nor did
your fathers know, that He might make you know that
man shall not live by bread alone; but man lives by
every word that proceeds from the mouth of the LORD.

—Deuteronomy 8:2–3

— SUGGESTED READING: EXODUS 13:14–22; 14; 16; 17;
DEUTERONOMY 1; 8; 9; 10 —

The bumper sticker "Not all who wander are lost"
makes me smile. I've done my share of wandering. A
couple of summers ago, two friends and I went on a hike in
the mountains while our husbands golfed. As we trudged
along with our backpacks, we congratulated each other on
being so adventurous. As I had hiked that trail before, I
confidently led the way up through the tall stands of
Douglas firs as we walked and walked. *And* walked. It had

been a hard winter; the heavy snows and the spring runoff had changed some of the creeks, and the familiar path was now not so familiar.

After several hours, we were hungry and tired, and instead of reaching our destination of the meadow where we were to have lunch as we enjoyed the glorious view, we were sitting on a log surrounded by dense forest, munching our turkey sandwiches, swatting mosquitoes, and debating what to do. "We can't be lost," I argued, "we've just gone a bit out of our way." Quite a bit. Thanks to the guidance of a fellow hiker (who informed us we were on the Pacific Crest Trail headed for Canada), we finally got on the right path. We have a great snapshot of us at the trail's fork, all of us pointing different directions.

But I doubt the children of Israel found their wandering to be humorous, and while they weren't lost, they couldn't seem to get where they needed to go. They had a goal in mind; but the eleven-day journey turned into a forty-year saga. The book of Numbers, which helps to tell the story of the epic journey, has been described by the ancients as the "Book of Wanderings." They certainly did wander.

At first glance you wouldn't think the story of the children of Israel leaving Egypt to go back to Canaan would be relevant for us sophisticated people in this new millennium. And yet, human nature is the same; God is the same; and the truth is that sometimes the reason we are in a prolonged desert experience is due to our own disobedience, our own choices, our own attitudes.

There are six powerful principles about the desert of wandering that we can learn for our own lives:

SIX LESSONS LEARNED FROM
THE DESERT OF WANDERING

1. YOU MUST LEAVE EGYPT

> [Pharaoh said,] "Rise, go out from among my people,
> both you and the children of Israel. And go."
> —Exodus 12:31

As they left Egypt after the dramatic culmination of the plagues, instead of going through Philistine territory (which would have inevitably led to war), God led them a longer way through the desert and the Red Sea. He knew they'd be terrified by the Philistines and immediately want to go back to Egypt. Ultimately, they would have to confront their enemies, but God knew they weren't ready yet (see Ex. 13:17). It was challenge enough getting out of Egypt—getting "Egypt" out of their thinking, their behavior. After all, they'd lived there as a nation-within-a-nation for four hundred years, almost twice as long as America is old. They hadn't started out as slaves; they'd been privileged guests of Joseph, the second most powerful man in the nation. But after Joseph died, things slowly changed until the once-honored and strong people were enslaved.

Recently, I was involved with a conference at a women's prison. I met many talented, intelligent women whose lives and potential have been indelibly marked by sin. Not one of those women ever started out in childhood to be in that place; but slowly—often due to drugs and alcohol—many of them became enslaved. Sin is a cruel taskmaster. Many of the women accepted Jesus into their lives, but it will take time for them to become free, spiritually and every other way. The children of Israel needed a dramatic deliverance in order to propel them out of Egypt, and some of us do, too.

The Israelites were absolutely ingrained in Egypt—a very strong, educated, and sophisticated culture. And even though they were slaves, it was what they knew. The culture had influenced their thinking, influenced what they loved—good food, good times, worship of the golden calf, and debauched partying. And what should have been less than a two-week journey instead turned into a prolonged wandering in the desert. And all the adults over age twenty (except for Joshua and Caleb) never did enter Canaan.

On our way through to something better . . . what delays us, distracts us? Probably the same as the children of Israel: our creature comforts. Our desires, our needs, our hungers. Assurances that everything's going to be all right, that none of us will be hurt. That we all will be able to do what we want and stay happy. But in order to grab on to the next step that God has for us—we need to let go of the old life.

To depart is to die a little. But to stay is to die a little, too . . . One must have a place before one can give it up. One must receive before giving, exist before abandoning oneself in faith. We receive a place only so as eventually to leave it, treasure only so as to cast it away, a personal existence only so as to be able to offer it up.

— PAUL TOURNIER, *A Place for You*[1]

―◇―

2. YOUR ANSWER MAY LIE WITHIN YOUR OBSTACLE

The children of Israel lifted their eyes, and behold, the Egyptians marched after them. So they were very afraid . . . And Moses said to the people, "Do not be afraid. Stand still, and see the salvation of the LORD" . . . Then Moses stretched out his hand over the sea; and the LORD . . . made the sea into dry land.

— Exodus 14:10, 13, 21

When the children of Israel left Egypt, they thought they had escaped oppression — until they got to the Red Sea, and realized Pharaoh's army was behind them. What to do? They were trapped. Stuck. Pharaoh thought surely he would capture his escaping workforce and said, "They are bewildered by the land; the wilderness has closed them in" (Ex.14:3).

But the Red Sea, which was the children of Israel's obstacle, became their very means of deliverance. The answer was right under their noses — they just had to see it with eyes of faith and obey God. When they marched out onto dry land

and the waters closed back over the Egyptian army, Miriam picked up the tambourine and led them in a song: "Sing to the LORD, for He has triumphed gloriously!" (Ex. 15:21).

I know what it feels like to be "bewildered by the land" and "closed in." But I'm learning it really isn't the circumstance as much as how I see it. When I look at what seems to be an impossible situation through God's eyes I see it in a different light. At His leading, I can move toward it rather than escape from it or panic. Right now in my life I am in that "empty nest" phase—a place I've dreaded. Even the sound of it has overtones of "life is over," "I'm finished," and other equally depressing thoughts. And yet I am seeing that as I am released from hands-on mothering, I now have the time to write, to think. So what was empty has become a place of fulfillment. I've found that when I am in a desert place of emptiness, yes, of wandering, it often precedes a new, wonderful place. As I look back upon my life, every time God has emptied my hands He has filled them with something better. Yes, there have been times of waiting. Sometimes almost a panic—now what? There have been times when I have felt stuck—boxed in by circumstances. And yet, if I am patient and wait on God within that situation, He delivers me.

What is your "Red Sea"? Don't run from it; instead, as Moses said, "Stand still, and see the salvation of the LORD, which He will accomplish for you today . . . The LORD will fight for you, and you shall hold your peace" (Ex. 14:13–14).

Near us the beautiful Three Sisters mountains tower

over us—named by the early settlers Faith, Hope and Charity. The mountain passes now are well marked; the roads are paved and well traveled. But in 1853, a wagon train tried to find the pass they'd heard could save them many miles to the famous Willamette Valley.

Unfortunately, the leader of the train had no idea where he was going, so instead of waiting to make sure they were following the right trail, they forged their way west, getting hopelessly lost.[2]

They wandered in the chilling rain without proper food and many died due to starvation and the cold weather. Now as I look at that middle mountain—Hope—I'm reminded that there is a mountain pass through there. What looked like an insurmountable obstacle to those dear people really was the way through.

There is a way—but it's important to know that whoever you are following has been there before you and that you're on the right trail.

Madame Guyon wrote many centuries ago:

> Courage, dear soul. You have come to the edge of the Red Sea, where soon you will see the enemy receive his reward. Follow on your present path. Remain immovable, like a rock. Do not find a pretext to stir from where you are . . . the Lord will fight for you now. Many people break down at this place. They do not find the way out. They stop here and never advance . . . That which is a rock of destruction to

others is the port of safety to such a one . . . You must
know that in all the many states that are involved in
the interior life, each new stage, each new level, is pre-
ceded by a sacrifice. Then comes an abandon, and following that is always a state of utter destitution . . .
[and] . . . Abandoned ones are praising ones.[3]

3. THANK GOD FOR HIS PROVISION (NO MATTER WHAT)

Do all things without complaining and disputing.

—Philippians 2:14

In everything give thanks; for this is the will of God in
Christ Jesus for you.

—1 Thessalonians 5:18

My husband and I know that God has been nudging us
in the direction of selling the house we have lived in for
twenty-two years so that we can do more ministry-oriented
things without having to bring in a certain income. I love this
house. I love its memories. It's big; it's beautiful. But we know
it's time to let it go. I have to confess that sometimes I understand the Israelites all too well. When I read in Scripture that
they wanted to go back to Egypt for the garlic, the leeks, and
the figs, I was amazed. *They'd rather have exotic food and be a
slave? How base,* I thought. And yet I know that feeling. As
noble as I want to be, I like the *stuff.* And when the stuff
needs to go, I complain. Maybe not by so many words, but
by my attitude. How deeply Egypt can get ingrained in us.

It is taking me a lifetime to develop a spirit of thanks that says, "God, I give You thanks—in everything." When we do this, we are making a very simple but profound statement. We are saying, "God, You are. You are Lord of my life, and You are in control." That means being thankful for the food; for the circumstances; for the people in my life; for the spiritual leadership God has provided.

Being grateful doesn't come naturally to a lot of us. Our natural person wants what we deserve—we have our rights, and when we don't get them, we can really complain. Some of us have complaining honed to an art form. I have a button that's a good reminder: "The more you complain, the longer God lets you live." But if we can develop a thankful heart where we are, we unlock a life-changing dynamic principle.

Maybe you're saying, "I know I should be thankful, but things are tough right now. I just can't." Psalm 42:8 says, "The LORD will command His lovingkindness in the daytime, and in the night His song shall be with me." Sometimes you need to sing in the nighttime, even if you are afraid, even if your faith is weak. We can choose to be thankful even if we don't feel thankful. As Catherine Marshall wrote, "Praising God in tough situations is like developing a photo negative: You take the negative things of life and plunge them into the positive solution of the Presence of God; because the Lord inhabits the praises of His people. And in His Presence is fullness of joy."[4]

God takes us step-by-step. He knows what we can handle

today. Mark 10:32 says that as Jesus' disciples followed, they were afraid. The point was that they followed Him, even if they were afraid. First take the step; let Jesus handle the fear. If we have a heart that says, "Yes, God, I trust You— even though this may be a very difficult place. My marriage may be painful; I may be having problems with my children; I hate this job; our finances are impossible." And He says, "Will you give thanks here? Will you let Me be God here?"

And we can say, "Yes," or we can keep trying to arrange the perfect situation for ourselves, to stay safe. Comfortable. Becoming thankful means letting go— letting go of expectations; letting go of trying to control.

When we begin to thank God for His provision in that place of wandering, something wonderful happens. The bitter waters become sweet. The manna comes down. We are nourished daily and led.

If we could see beneath the surface of many a life, we would see that thousands of people within the Church are suffering spiritually from "arrested development;" they never reach spiritual maturity; they never do all the good they were intended to do; and this is due to the fact that at some point in their lives they refused to go further; some act of self-sacrifice was required of them, and they felt they could not and would not make it; some habits had to be given up, some personal relation altered and renounced, and they

refused to take the one step which would have opened
up for them a new and vital development.

—OLIVE WYON[5]

<hr />

God has two dwellings—one in heaven and the other
in a thankful heart.

—IZAAK WALTON

<hr />

4. YOUR WORSHIP HAS CONSEQUENCES

See, I am setting before you today a blessing and a
curse—the blessing if you obey the commands of the
LORD your God that I am giving you today; the curse
if you disobey the commands of the LORD your God
and turn from the way that I command you today by
following other gods, which you have not known.

—Deuteronomy 11:26–28 NIV

First there was the incident at the foot of Mount Sinai.
Moses was up on the mountain having an encounter with
God, receiving the Ten Commandments. It took a few
weeks though, and the people got impatient. So they crafted
a golden calf and began worshiping it. It is astounding to
think how they could enter into idol worship so soon after
God delivered them from the Red Sea, and yet their base
desires and fears prevailed.

Years later, after the Israelites' triumphant march across

Jordan into the promised land, they had a great victory at Jericho. And then as they went on to Ai—an insignificant little city—they were defeated. Whipped. Joshua was humiliated by this turn of events. "Why, God?" he asked.

Later it was discovered that Achan of the tribe of Judah had disobeyed God—he'd hidden some pagan treasures and money in his tent, and his disobedience carried enormous consequences for them all. Years before, the children of Israel had painful lessons in the wilderness about obedience. And yet here they were, defeated again—even after getting into the promised land (see Josh. 6–8).

The point is, in the arid place of wandering, be careful what you worship; what you take into your tent, your life. Our wounds and needs can take on an acute sense of urgency in the desert. It is essential that we be aware that our hearts are prone to wander, and bring our needs to God to be met in His way, His timing. Otherwise, we are in a dangerous place of disobedience. And disobedience to God has consequences, sooner or later.

I have a friend who is unhappy in her marriage. She is contemplating finding sweet release in the arms of another. She is at a critical point, and I long for her to know that the path she is contemplating is an illusion. She knows what is right, but only she can turn and say, "Let God deal with it."

It hurts to honestly look at our deepest struggle, our deepest need—the pain is real. We are in agony. We are tempted to numb it with sex, alcohol, food, materialism, or some ego trip and then take the substitute into the core of our lives to pacify the hurt, refusing to see what our actions are doing to us and to those who love us. But when we throw our broken selves back on Him and say, "Forgive me, Father . . . You promised to meet my every need according to Your riches in glory," He does meet us. And rather than this being a place of defeat—as it was for Joshua at Ai—it can be a place of victory. Walking with an awareness of our very real needs can make us stronger, more compassionate.

Some of our wandering may be the result of others' disobedience, or unfinished business from long ago. Because of Joseph's older brothers' sin, he was sold into Egypt. And when the Israelites left, they carried Joseph's bones with them back to Canaan—as Joseph had requested when he was dying. I wonder who had the task of carrying Joseph's bones around the desert for forty years! Some of us are carrying around a lot of old bones from long ago—from other people. It's called "baggage," and we need to let go.

In Numbers 20, there is an instance when the people were desperately thirsty and were complaining again to Moses. And it wasn't just the fact of no water. They were also unhappy that there were no pomegranates, or figs, or vines. God told Moses to go to a rock and speak to it before the people, and the rock would bring forth water. But Moses' patience was gone, and he angrily struck the rock instead of speaking to it. This act of disobedience caused God not to bring Moses into the promised land.

As I read this I thought, *This seems a bit harsh, God, after all Moses has gone through with leading Your people out of Egypt. He didn't want the job in the first place, but You convinced him he could do it. So after all their complaining and whining, he struck the rock in the wilderness and water poured out. But You were so displeased that You decided Moses should die in the wilderness and never cross over the Jordan River to Canaan. Why?*

As I analyze this passage, maybe God was saying: "Moses—after all we've been through, can't you let Me be God at this point? Why do you have to take matters into your own hands? *You* are not God! You can't change these people. I know they're a pain in the neck. But all I'm asking you to do is speak My words to the rock. Let Me produce the results."

Perhaps our greatest sin is that we do not wholly trust, wholly believe our Source. Maybe it comes out of selfishness—or out of a belief that we are the ones fighting the battle. People follow Christ for their own reasons. Some follow because they are afraid. Others follow because they need Him. Some follow for the miracles. Ask yourself: *Why am I following Him? Can I leave results in God's hands—and simply obey Him?*

In our culture, often the test of what is important is, "If it works." God has a different standard: "Is it true?" Truth is enough. God will handle the consequences.

There are two things to do about the Gospel—believe it and behave it.

—SUSANNA WESLEY (1669–1742),[6]
MOTHER OF JOHN AND CHARLES WESLEY

---

5. HE NEVER STOPS CARING FOR YOU—EVEN IN YOUR WANDERING

> Blessed is the man whose strength is in You,
> Whose heart is set on pilgrimage.
>
> —Psalm 84:5

So . . . daily manna is enough in the desert. Daily. We don't need to know what's around the corner. The Lord Himself taught us to pray, "Give us this day our daily bread." God was so provoked by the people's complaining and disobedience that He threatened to kill all of them in the wilderness, but Moses interceded, quoting God's very words back to Him. This is a powerful reminder of the importance of intercessory prayer as Moses' intercession saved his people more than once.

In all their wandering through the desert, God still cared for the Israelites, and He never left them. He still provided manna and quail. He gave them laws that helped to protect them and build their society. He didn't let their shoes or clothes wear out as they wearily trudged through the land. He patiently taught them amazing, incredible lessons of faith and trust. And He says to us as well, "I will never leave you nor forsake you."

Even in our wandering, our confusing delays and detours, God doesn't leave us. He restores and nourishes and speaks to us right where we are. In knowing His Word and worshiping Him, we are restored, and He hides us in the cleft of the rock in a dry and thirsty land and speaks to us, giving us strength to go on.

His Word will nourish us in those places, and we can be assured that if we choose to trust Him, there is a plan. We are going somewhere — eventually! There will be victory — eventually! And though we may get tired of the "same-old, same-old" nourishment, it is nourishment. It may not be glamorous; it may mean just putting one foot in front of the other, obeying, trusting. If we're going to cross over into the promised land, we cannot flirt with God. Our attitude toward Him has to be wholehearted, submissive, willing to obey. No other idols, no other loves.

As we follow — are we being led by our hungers and desires, our pride, our sense of security? Or are we learning to follow because He is God and there is none other?

The desert initiates us into the life of the spirit by helping us to discover who we most deeply are. To follow Christ means that we must let go of excessive attachments . . . Christ asks us to abandon our idols, whatever they may be, and to love Him with our entire being.

— ANDREW MURRAY,
With Christ in the School of Prayer

---

6. WHEN IT'S TIME—TAKE A STEP OF FAITH

You have dwelt long enough at this mountain. Turn,
and take your journey . . . Look, the LORD your God
has set the land before you; go up and possess it . . .
do not fear or be discouraged.

—Deuteronomy 1:6–7, 21

What finally ends the wandering? A goal; a destination; a
vision of what's possible. Ever since I can remember, I've had
a dream to write. *Someday* . . . said the longing deep inside of
me, *I'll be a writer.* I kept diaries and journals all through
school, into college and marriage. Then, I quit. The early marriage years were hectic, and my dream got shelved for a while,
until one night. We had just moved with our small sons. The
children were asleep and Bill was at a meeting as I was sorting through boxes, putting things away. That's when I came
across them—my journals, an odd assortment of notebooks
and diaries in the bottom of a box. I remember hugging them
to myself like long-lost children, crying. *Where have you been?
I've missed you so!* It was like finding my dream again. Here was
concrete evidence that once I'd dreamed of being a writer.

There have been other dreams. Twenty years ago, I
remember seeing a street person, a young woman. The look
on her face shook me; the deadness, the blank expression.
She is lost, I heard His still, small voice say. *Lost.* It was an
electric moment. I wondered, *How do I reach that woman for*

Christ? I could not get her face out of my mind. That experience helped motivate *Virtue* magazine's ministry to women in prison. Whenever I feel discouraged or want to quit working in the prison, I see her face again, and remember, *There is a way to reach her.*

I've pursued some dreams I shouldn't have and plunged into projects that seemed good, only to find myself wandering, feeling like a failure. Later, I had to admit that I hadn't really waited to see if this was the right thing to do. I've often done something because it was a good idea; because it worked for someone else; and I thought others expected it of me.

The question to ask is this: Is my dream . . . God's dream? If God is in this opportunity—if it is compatible with the gifts that He has given us; if it is consistent with His Word; if it is in His timing—then we can proceed. And perhaps there is a place in our journey with God where He trusts us with a dream. Is it scary to take faith opportunities? Absolutely. Fear is powerful and often drowns out the voice of faith as we are tempted to believe the negative report: "Awfully big giants out there" . . . "Possibility of failure" . . . "Big-time defeat!"

But God will lead us only when we are ready to go on. Only when, knowing our complete dependence upon Him, we believe. To "possess the land" means to take a risk—to step out and follow His still, small voice and not worry about the results. It can be scary to take steps that involve risk, but in each new area of life there are many opportunities to be afraid. If we allow it, fear can dominate our lives. But there are also many faith opportunities, and when we learn to listen to Him and risk saying "yes," it will be all right.

We cross over from wandering into purpose by cultivating an attitude that says, "God, thank You—right here, right now! In my anxieties . . . in my need . . . . You are awesome in this place!" And indeed He is.

What is needed in spiritual matters is reckless abandonment to the Lord Jesus Christ, reckless and uncalculating abandonment, with no reserve anywhere about it; not sad, you cannot be sad if you are abandoned absolutely.

—OSWALD CHAMBERS, *Conformed to His Image*[8]

— REFLECTION —

There are times to take steps of faith, to believe. Sometimes it means taking a risk through deep waters, not being sure of the future. What does it mean for you to "take possession of the land," to enter a new level of faith? Write some "spiritual goals" for yourself; put them in a sealed envelope; tuck them away somewhere to be opened at a later date.

— PRAYER —

Father, you alone know what lies before me this day,
grant that in every hour of it I may stay close to you.
Let me today embark on no undertaking that is not in
line with your will for my life, nor shrink from any
sacrifice which your will may demand. Suggest,
direct, control every movement of my mind; for my
Lord Christ's sake. Amen.

—JOHN BAILLIE, *A Diary of Private Prayer*[9]

We grow spiritually by obeying God through the
words of Jesus being made spirit and life to us, and
by paying attention to where we are, not to whether
we are growing or not. We grow spiritually as our
Lord grew physically, by a life of simple, unobtrusive
obedience.

—OSWALD CHAMBERS, *My Utmost for His Highest*[10]

7

THE DESERT OF DEPRESSION

And now my heart is broken. Depression haunts my
days. My weary nights are filled with pain as though
something were relentlessly gnawing at my bones.

—Job 30:16 NLT

— SUGGESTED READING: COLOSSIANS 3:1–17; PHILIPPIANS 4:4–9 —

It's difficult to go back now, to remember what it was
like. As I reflect on that time of depression, I had no
clear understanding of why I was going through it; I only
knew that somehow life had lost its meaning and there were
times I felt I couldn't go on. I was tempted by thoughts of
suicide, and while I couldn't do that to my family, I thought
maybe they'd be better off without me.

I could put a label on what I was experiencing—depression

brought about by a collision of reality and expectations, compounded by physical illness, loss, and burnout. But the label trivializes the hollowness and depths of despair that I was feeling. There are many causes for depression, including physical illness or a chemical imbalance in the body, and there are some unknown causes. However, there is much help available for depression, and we don't need to suffer needlessly. Medication may be helpful; therapy may be helpful. Certainly prayer is a powerful weapon against depression.

What is depression? We all have "depressing" days at times, but usually the feeling passes. When it doesn't—as it didn't in my case—it can become depression. Its symptoms often include the following:

- A generalized sad or numb feeling, such that you do not enjoy normal activities;
- Loss of appetite;
- Difficulty in sleeping;
- Physical signs such as dizziness, headaches;
- Irritability, crying for no evident reason, difficulty making decisions;
- Withdrawal from contact with others;
- Decreased sexual interest.[1]

Outwardly, I functioned: wife of a busy publisher; mother of five handsome and vital children; leader in church activities. One day I gave a luncheon in my home, and a friend told me later that as she drove home with another friend who had attended the luncheon, the woman remarked, "Nancie has the perfect life. I wish I could be like her."

Need comes not from discovering Christ's all-sufficiency; it comes from stumbling upon our own insufficiency . . . Spiritual need is rooted in our honesty.

—CALVIN MILLER, *Walking with Saints*[2]

THE PERFECT LIFE

The problem with a perfect life is that it doesn't exist, even though I fully intended to have one. I married at age eighteen after one year of college to a wonderful man, and although I was young, Bill was five years older than I and out of school, and I thought I was ready for life. I had always loved learning and had been an honor student in high school, but after we married, Bill enrolled in graduate school so I got a job to help him get through. I put my schooling on hold, thinking I would come back to it someday.

Life just began happening to me. Bill finished graduate school. We had our first child, took a position in a church. After eight years we had four healthy and handsome sons, all this time involved in pastoring and missions work. Bill started a magazine for a missions organization and realized he had found a niche that challenged his entrepreneurial and organizational skills. With my love for writing, I was right beside him, doing book reviews and articles—meanwhile juggling the home front. To say life was busy would be an understatement.

We decided to give publishing our full efforts and moved to a beautiful little mountain community to begin our own publishing venture. Our plan was to "simplify life"—cut our own wood; I would make homemade soup on our woodstove and give our growing family quality time. And at first, it was an idyllic existence. Our family—which now included our daughter, Amy, adopted from Korea—was sheltered and protected in the small community. The only problem with escaping to the woods was that we took ourselves with us, and before too many years, we had three magazines and a staff of more than forty people.

PHYSICAL AND EMOTIONAL PAIN

As I mentioned in Chapter 3, shortly after we adopted Amy, I acquired toxic shock syndrome. Besides a painfully slow recovery period and the attending depression, I was overwhelmed by feelings of loss. My children were growing up and it was evident that eventually they, too, would leave. My mother was dying. Besides my own trips to the doctor, I hadn't planned on the countless treks Amy and I needed to make to special tutors, speech therapists, the ophthalmologist, and the dentist as it was dawning on us that she had many special needs.

So in the midst of what looked on the outside like a very full and good life, I was feeling more and more exhausted and disillusioned. I had put all my emotional well-being into my parents, my husband, and my children, and they weren't coming through for me.

Medication did seem to help some, but I didn't connect my emotional state to my physical condition. To this day I don't know if my physical illness caused my depression or if the depression was caused by my physical illness. Regardless, they were related. My nerves and emotions were raw, although at times I'd be all right when I was distracted by a project or surrounded by people. Then when I was still, I would hear the inner noise of agony and desperation.

Solitude and journaling my dark thoughts became a catharsis, but I often wondered if that was even healthy. As Anne Lamott puts it, "My mind remains a bad neighborhood that I don't like to go into alone."[3] Depression would periodically descend on me like a black cloud, but through determined Scripture memorization I fought back as much as possible. I would go on solitary walks and recite: "Create in me a clean heart, O God . . . Renew a right spirit within me . . . Unto Thee, O Lord, do I lift up my soul . . . I can do all things through Christ who strengthens me." I would ask myself: *I have so much to be thankful for. Why am I so miserable?*

I was convinced no one worked as hard as I did just to be normal. Now as I watch family videos of that time, I look like an efficient machine on autopilot, my face like a mask. I had found an identity in what I could "produce." And produce I did, until I got sick. I'd had boundless energy to do my responsibilities and do them well: prepare meals, entertain, get to the kids' basketball games, teach Bible study, write articles, and speak at women's events. Who I was had been so defined as "wife of Bill," "mother of Jon, Eric, Chris, Andy, and Amy," "magazine editor," all of which I loved and would still tell you that's all I ever really wanted, but now as I sank into an emotional abyss, I felt lost. I felt like saying to God, "What do You want from me, too? You, who are standing a distance away, detached, arms folded, watching? Do I have to dance a certain way, perform well — get a smattering of applause . . . then do it again (trying, trying, trying to please You)?" I really think that at the heart of it, I was angry that my performance hadn't brought me acceptance. It was futile — I could never be good enough.

I understood exactly what author Lewis Smedes meant when he wrote,

> "Guilt was not my problem as I felt it. What I felt most was a glob of unworthiness that I could not tie down to any concrete sins I was guilty of. What I needed more than pardon was a sense that God accepted me, owned me, held me, affirmed me, and would never let go of me even if he was not too impressed with what he had on his hands."[4]

I kept coming back to this one thought: *Why can't I be loved just for being me?* It was a deep, primal emotion, and with the question, I smothered back sobs. I kept thinking if

I could find a private altar somewhere and find God, He would hear me and hold me. I just couldn't get there.

He is the source of all peace. Where is this peace to be found? In our own weakness, in those places where we feel most broken, most insecure, most in agony, most afraid.

—HENRI NOUWEN[5]

SEVEN REASONS FOR DEPRESSION; SEVEN RESPONSES

Although some of us are more prone to depression, we are not victims—we have an effective weapon at our disposal: We can choose our response. I believe that much of my depression was caused by my lack of assertiveness, and things began to turn around for me when I began to consciously choose my responses to situations. It is important to emphasize here that you should not hesitate to get professional help from the right professional. If you broke a leg, you wouldn't see a dentist. Jesus said, "Those who are well have no need of a physician, but those who are sick" (Matt. 9:12). You may need to consult a professional who can help you understand what is going on.

What helped me more than anything was realizing that I had a twisted view of God and grace, and as I gained a clearer understanding from God's Word of how my responses could change life's stressful situations, my depression lifted. Here are seven examples in the Bible of people who were afflicted by depression, their responses, and the consequences of those responses.

1. DEPRESSION FROM ANGER (WHAT WE CAN LEARN FROM CAIN—GENESIS 4:2–7)

> Now Abel kept flocks, and Cain worked the soil. In the course of time Cain brought some of the fruits of the soil as an offering to the LORD. But Abel brought fat portions from some of the firstborn of his flock. The LORD looked with favor on Abel and his offering, but on Cain and his offering he did not look with favor. So Cain was very angry, and his face was downcast. Then the LORD said to Cain, "Why are you angry? Why is your face downcast? If you do what is right, will you not be accepted? But if you do not do what is right, sin is crouching at your door; it desires to have you, but you must master it." (Gen. 4:2–7 NIV)

Cain had an opportunity to master his anger, but he went the other direction instead and ended up killing his own brother. As I read this story I thought, *Surely I have nothing in common with this awful man.* However, the truth is that I do. Cain didn't deal with his anger—he internalized it, and it smoldered into rage, which he finally took out on his

126

brother. While I didn't direct anger onto other people, I turned it inward, and depression is often caused by anger turned inward. Cain was trying to approach God on his own terms. And I, too, was trying to come to God on my own terms, with my own works—clearly an unacceptable sacrifice. I desperately needed to understand grace.

It was humbling for me to swallow my pride and talk to a counselor who could give me insight and perspective I wouldn't get anywhere else. And yet it was important because I took time to ask, *Why do I drive myself so? Why do I have this underlying anger?*

I was angry at the futility of it all. If my efforts weren't producing the right results, why keep trying? The voice of the taskmaster, "Do more, pray more, do it better," was not God's voice. But this voice was difficult to argue with because it seemed that it was pushing me to do good things. How could good things be bad? As I saw how my negative, condemning self-talk was contributing to my mental despair, I began memorizing verses about grace, often seeing them as though for the first time. *By grace am I saved through faith—not of works, lest I boast.* Grace means *not* of myself. It is God's gift—with no strings!

It took me a while to admit that I was angry. I had been raised to believe that good Christians don't get angry. I do not recall my father ever raising his voice, not once (this was a man with seven children!), although he had subtle ways of expressing anger. How like my father I tend to be! When my mother would try to discuss a conflict with him, he'd just walk out of the house. Of course, I married a man who quite freely and openly expresses his anger while I swallow mine, avoiding conflict at all costs. I am learning the importance of honest and loving confrontation, especially with close family members.

"Be angry, and do not sin," Paul said (Eph. 4:26). Anger is a powerful emotion, but if we can express it in a healthy and assertive way, we can let it go. It's when we internalize it that it contributes to depression. I was becoming aware that the continual, inward condemnation I was inflicting on myself was harmful. First John 3:20 says, "For if our heart condemns us, God is greater than our heart, and knows all things." I needed God to be greater than my heart.

I wrote this prayer in my journal:

> *God, how I need a fresh baptism of Your love and grace. I cannot do one more thing without You. I cannot love in my self. Help me put away childish things. I do not want to be a little girl achieving and performing to be noticed. By grace I am saved. O God, don't let me put my perfectionism on my children. Help me to look into their eyes, their faces, and let them know I love them. Not for what they do, but for who they are.*

2. Depression from Satanic Attacks (What We Can Learn from Saul—1 Samuel 16:14–23)

There is an enemy of our souls. Satan intends for us to be destroyed, our effectiveness ruined. Saul was afflicted by evil spirits that were fed by his own insecurities, arrogance, and jealousy. Although he asked David the psalmist to sing to him to soothe his spirit, his mental condition ultimately destroyed him. It's fascinating to think that most likely some of our most beloved psalms—the Twenty-third and others like it—were probably sung to Saul by David. Did Saul respond to God? It would seem not.

Our daughter, Amy, had some deep and stubborn wounds from being abandoned as a child, and when she was in her senior year of high school, she began having troubling, vivid nightmares about her birth mother leaving her. She sank into a suicidal depression as evil thoughts and images appeared to her at night, disturbing her sleep. I believe the timing was no accident, as Amy had made a commitment to become a Christian and was planning to get baptized. What all of us went through that final week before she was baptized was like nothing we have ever experienced.

One night after we came home from church, Amy began screaming hateful, awful things about herself and how she wanted to die. She ran upstairs, and we heard her in her third-floor bedroom, pounding her head against the wall. I was about to call 911 because I thought she was having some kind of psychotic episode, but Bill and I looked at each other and realized this was a spiritual battle. Satan was going all out not to lose that girl. But he did, praise God!

We went up to her room, and both of us held Amy in our arms and prayed intensely for three hours against the enemy. I don't know how else to describe what happened except that Amy had a dramatic deliverance, and she was filled with joy. She laughed and praised God. It was an amazing evening in the Carmichael household, to say the least. She said, "I need to burn some things," and dug around in her drawer for some of her journals that had contained her dark thoughts. The next week she was baptized, and spiritual ground was established in Amy's life that continues to be an unfolding miracle nearly a year later. We are also grateful that during this time Amy was under the care of a Christian psychologist who lovingly and prayerfully helped her deal with her anger at being abandoned as a child.

How amazing that God does speak to us in our difficult places—but it takes courage and willingness to listen. How essential it is to meditate on Scripture and study it to get an accurate picture of God as we are vulnerable to other voices in the desert as well. Satan came to Jesus in the desert, urging Him to turn the stones into bread, yet Jesus answered him with the Word of God and triumphed in that place.

3. DEPRESSION FROM BITTERNESS (WHAT WE CAN LEARN FROM MICHAL—2 SAMUEL 6:1–23)

Read this story and you'll see the truth—Michal was *used* as a pawn by her father as well as by David. And yet her hurt hardened into cold anger, eventually becoming bitterness. And in the long run, it did her in—she ended up being barren.

One afternoon I listened to a friend pour out her anger and frustration. She'd been wounded by fellow Christians; she was disappointed in her daughter; she'd been hurt by a pastor's inconsistency. Her once-soft features and eyes had a hardness to them as her quiet words fell like acid rain. My heart broke to see my friend tortured like this as I remembered her once-optimistic laughter. She had become bitter, and it was not good to see. What had happened?

Michal, the daughter of King Saul, had once been in love with David, but now, seeing him dancing in front of the ark of the covenant as it was brought back home to Jerusalem, she was filled with contempt. When David came up to bless his own family, she greeted him with sarcasm: "How glorious was the king of Israel today, uncovering himself today in the eyes of the maids of his servants!" (2 Sam. 6:20). What had happened to turn love into bitterness? Yes, Michal had been used, hurt, and betrayed. Was it right? No. But Scripture says that Michal remained barren the rest of her life.

The point is, bitterness is nasty stuff, and it can choke the life out of us if we don't keep short accounts. Our responses to the wrongs in our lives determine whether or not we will go on to more productive lives or barren lives. We must honestly acknowledge the offenses that come to us and then let them go. Forgive because Jesus forgives us — not because the offender deserves it — seventy times seven, if necessary.

4. DEPRESSION FROM LOSS (WHAT WE CAN LEARN FROM JOB — JOB 1–3)

It's not hard to understand why Job was depressed. After all, he lost everything that was dear to him (except his nagging wife)! What is inspiring is to see how he worked through his losses with honesty and openness. If we live long enough, life will present us with losses, and there doesn't seem to be any formula for who suffers loss when or how much, although Job's friends tried to convince him there was one.

A lot of my own depression was caused by my not taking time to grieve my father's death—like anger, I swallowed it. Other losses began accumulating in my life as well and showed up as depression.

When I finally acknowledged my losses and learned to worship God there—thanking Him for what I had, not blaming Him for what I didn't have—the sense of loss was replaced by gratitude. Job's healing was complete when God restored him as he worshiped and prayed for his friends. It is healing to extend compassion to others out of our own experience.

Life is short, and we have never too much time for gladdening the hearts of those who are traveling the dark journey with us. Oh, be swift to love, make haste to be kind!

—HENRI F. AMIEL, *Journal*[6]

---

5. DEPRESSION FROM GUILT (WHAT WE CAN LEARN FROM DAVID—2 SAMUEL 11–12)

After David finally confronted his sin by talking it out with Nathan the prophet, he repented and asked forgiveness.

Still, the consequences of his sin were very real as Nathan told him that "the sword [would] never depart from his [David's] house" and adversity would come against him from his own family. Furthermore, Nathan told David, his son with Bathsheba would not live. When the child became ill, David got on his face before God, fasting and weeping, pleading for his son's life. But after the child died, David got up, washed and anointed himself, changed his clothes, and went into the house of the Lord to worship. Although the consequences of his sin would impact him always, David was restored, and said, "While the child was alive, I fasted and wept . . . But now he is dead; why should I fast? Can I bring him back again? I shall go to him, but he shall not return to me" (2 Sam. 12:22–23).

Sometimes we need to find safe places to talk some things out. Depression can be caused from guilt. Drs. Minirth and Meier say this:

> Some situations that undermine our self-esteem are self-inflicted and the result of sin. We may see ourselves as people of integrity and good moral behavior until we have an extramarital affair or cheat someone in a business deal. At that moment, we ought to feel defiled and unworthy, and our self-esteem should be diminished until we have repented, made amends, and made sure (by placing ourselves in an accountable relationship) that we will not do it again.
>
> Sometimes a Christian comes into the clinic for

treatment of depression and says, "I don't know why I'm depressed. My business is going well, my spouse and I aren't engaged in any conflict, my kids are doing well at home and at school, my health is fine—and yet I've been depressed for two months." We then ask, "What have you been doing these past two months that might be making you depressed?'" At this, the client will often get a surprised, "how-did-you-read-my-mind" sort of look and say (guiltily), "Well, the truth is . . . I have sort of been having, like, well, an affair, you know, but gee, I didn't think something like that could have anything to do with depression . . . could it?" Indeed it could, and it often does. But after confessing and repenting of sin, and receiving God's forgiveness and forgiving oneself, the depression usually goes away.[7]

6. DEPRESSION FROM LOW SELF-ESTEEM (WHAT WE CAN LEARN FROM LEAH—GENESIS 29:16–35)

Leah had been told all her life she was not as beautiful or as worthy as her younger sister, Rachel. Her father had pity on her though, and deceived Jacob, sending Leah into his wedding tent. In the morning, Jacob realized he'd been tricked into marrying Leah first. Jacob did marry Rachel later, his true love. But poor Leah. Even though hers was the spectacular and worthy accomplishment of having three sons for Jacob, he still loved Rachel best. After every birth, she'd say, "Because the Lord has heard that I am unloved, He has therefore given me this son. Now perhaps my husband will love me." But finally, after she had her fourth son, Judah, she said: "Now I will praise Him." Judah means "praise." Leah gave up trying to win her husband's love and praised God where she was—in the midst of her imperfect situation.

Low self-esteem can certainly cause depression, but Leah did something very significant and helpful: She ultimately took responsibility for her own thinking about herself and her family. It can be hard to accept responsibility for our own depression—we let "life" and emotions happen to us, but we can choose our attitudes. It's ironic to note that at the end of Jacob's life, it was Leah he was buried next to, not Rachel (see Gen. 49:31).

How important it is to live from the center *out*. This takes some thinking, some quiet time. It was in the desert of depression where I was forced to take a hard look, to be thoughtful and intentional. There are three important principles in combating depression from low self-esteem: First, *do not compare yourself to anyone else; you are uniquely you.* Second, *praise God for who you are, where you are, what you have.* And third, *choose an attitude of gratefulness and thanksgiving to God in your situation.*

7. COMBATING DEPRESSION WITH FAITH (WHAT WE CAN LEARN FROM THE WOMAN WHO PRESSED THROUGH—MARK 5:25–34)

This story is about a woman who had a blood flow for years. Isolated and sick, she had desperately tried to get help from one doctor after another to no avail. But she set her faith upon Jesus and determined to press through what must have seemed insurmountable odds to touch Him, to receive healing. We, too, can determine to press through to touch Him, knowing He is our only hope; we can persevere to be well. Read chapter 3 of Colossians to see the importance of "setting" our minds on things above. It takes conscious choosing to "put on" positive faith attitudes and to "put off" negative, self-defeating attitudes. Philippians 4:4–8 says this:

> Rejoice in the Lord always. Again I will say, rejoice! Let your gentleness be known to all men. The Lord is at hand. Be anxious for nothing, but in everything by prayer and supplication, with thanksgiving, let your requests be made known to God; and the peace of God, which surpasses all understanding, will guard your hearts and minds through Christ Jesus. Finally, brethren, whatever things are true, whatever things are noble, whatever things are just, whatever things are pure, whatever things are lovely, whatever things are of good report, if there is any virtue and if there is anything praiseworthy—meditate on these things.

I memorized these scriptures and others like them to help counteract the voices of condemnation I was so used to absorbing. What we say to ourselves is influential. We can literally discourage our own selves or encourage ourselves. Jude 20 says, "Build yourselves up in your most holy faith" (NIV). We can help build a healthy self-esteem by encouraging ourselves to look to Him, again and again.

It was not easy for me to think in fresh patterns, to frame my thoughts in positive ways—to simply give myself a break. How did I get so down on myself? Of course it was legalistic thinking, false humility . . . not taking time to respect the heavy burden I was carrying with just caring for a family and a daughter with special needs. I found that keeping a good sense of humor is important, too. I realized that I was taking myself way too seriously.

The woman who pressed through to touch the hem of Jesus' garment was healed because she determined in her heart that if she could press through the crowd and just touch Jesus' garment, she would be healed. And she was. Jesus told her, "Your faith has made you whole."

---◆◇◆---

We are to be so deeply rooted in the love of Christ that we can stand up to any emotional earthquake, storm, or any form of discouragement. Knowing God as our Father also means to "grasp how wide and long and high and deep is the love of Christ, and to know this love that surpasses knowledge."

—JAMES HOUSTON, *The Transforming Friendship*[8]

---◆◇◆---

THE DEPRESSION IS TELLING
YOU SOMETHING

The longest journey is the journey inward.

—DAG HAMMARSKJOLD, *Markings*[9]

The overwhelming conviction that I didn't want to live anymore was absolutely right—I could not continue to live *that* way. I had to change or die. I've resigned myself to the fact that there will always be a tension in my life of weighing and sorting priorities. Life comes at all of us full force, and it is essential to protect ourselves by establishing and respecting boundaries, and to recognize buried emotions and deal with them.

Depression is not a tragedy. It actually can become a gift as we come to hear the truth of what God is saying to us about the way we are thinking and living. As I was confronted by what I viewed as the mess of my life, I became acquainted with the liberating grace of Jesus. In my weakness, He became strong. In my emptiness and confusion, He became my rock and purpose for living.

He turns a wilderness into pools of water,
And dry land into watersprings.
There He makes the hungry dwell,
That they may establish a city for a dwelling place,
And sow fields and plant vineyards,
That they may yield a fruitful harvest.

—PSALM 107:35–37

— REFLECTION —

Of the seven people in the Bible—Cain, Saul, Michal, Job, David, Leah, and the woman with the chronic illness—whose story do you most identify with at this time in your life? Using their example, how can you respond to God in a healing and cleansing way?

— PRAYER —

O Lord my God, when the storm is loud, and the night is dark, and the soul is sad, and the heart oppressed; then as a weary traveler, may I look to you; and beholding the light of your love, may it bear me on, until I learn to sing your song in the night. Amen.

—GEORGE DAWSON, *Little Book of Prayers*[10]

8

∾

THE DESERT OF LONELINESS

Turn to me and have mercy on me, for I am alone and
in deep distress.

—Psalm 25:16 NLT

— SUGGESTED READING: GENESIS 16; 21:1–21 —

I was seven months pregnant with our first child when
we had to move for my husband's new job. We left a
very busy and full life — Bill had been a youth pastor and a
student in graduate school; I had been working at an aero-
space company. Suddenly I was in a strange city and a
strange neighborhood with more time on my hands than I'd
ever had in my life. I got everything out of the boxes and
put away, the baby's room was ready, and the house was

clean. We had only one car so if I didn't take Bill to work, I was home alone and the day seemed to stretch out in front of me. My husband's parents were in the area, which was helpful for the weekends and evenings, but the days seemed endless.

I remember looking longingly out the window at the house across the street. My neighbor had a very active social life with people coming and going. One afternoon I decided to go introduce myself, so I took her a jar of my homemade jam. It was obvious that I needed her more than she needed me, as she brusquely said, "Thank you, nice to meet you," and went back inside.

I remember the acute feeling of rejection and loneliness. It was only for a short time as I soon got involved in the church and made friends. But I have never forgotten that feeling of isolation, of being set apart; the sense of being stuck on a plateau—alone. I didn't like it. Years later when we were pastoring, a single woman in our church, who had cared for her mother all her life, told me tearfully after her mother died, "I am just eaten up with loneliness." The desert of loneliness is not a pleasant place.

Loneliness is not the same as solitude. In our hectic lives, we must seek out occasional places of solitude. Jesus often got away to the seashore or the mountains to pray, and if God's Son needed to find quiet places, how much more do we need them? I've found that I need solitude to write and to think. This takes conscious choosing and I may have to miss some social events, especially if I have a writing project.

Loneliness, however, is thrust upon us. It may happen because we're in a certain place in life: after the death of a spouse, children leaving home, a move to a new area, illness, or a change in status. It may also come with a position of leadership or authority as it can be true that "it's lonely at the top"; no one knows the burdens a person bears even though he or she is surrounded by people.

Loneliness may be a result of our own choice not to open up to others, not to reach out. It may also come from laziness on our part, expecting others to call us instead of initiating the call. After all, we can't expect others to read our minds. And sometimes loneliness comes because we fear getting involved with others again if we've been hurt before, so we don't risk intimacy . . . and we are lonely.

WHAT WE CAN LEARN FROM HAGAR ABOUT LONELINESS (GENESIS 16; 21:1–21)

HAGAR WAS AN "OUTSIDER"

Hagar was a young Egyptian servant to Sarai, the beautiful wife of Abram. I read Hagar's story in several versions and my picture of her changed. I believe Hagar was no dowdy little servant girl. Where did she come from, anyway? Genesis 12:16 is a clue, as Abram and Sarai had gone to Egypt and Pharaoh had taken beautiful Sarai into his household. Abram had lied, telling Pharaoh she was his sister. Fortunately, God sent plagues on Pharaoh's house and he became aware that Sarai was Abram's wife. As Abram left Egypt, he was given much livestock, goods, and female servants. Most likely that's where Hagar entered the picture—no doubt young, beautiful, and sophisticated.

The years went by with Sarai and Abram remaining childless, even though God had promised they would have descendants as numerous as the sands of the sea. Sarai suggested that they take matters into their own hands and that Abram sleep with Hagar and have a child with her as a surrogate mother. Hagar must have been happy about being pregnant—it was probably a status-building thing for her and she most likely developed an attitude, intensifying her problems as the outsider. Sarai became jealous and began abusing Hagar, making her work harder and harder.

Finally Hagar couldn't stand it and ran away into the desert. Genesis 16 describes how an angel of the Lord found her beside a desert spring and asked her, "'Hagar, Sarai's servant, where have you come from, and where are you going?'" Then the angel told her, "the LORD has heard about your misery" (Gen. 16:11 NLT), and that she would have a son and more descendants than she could count. The angel also told Hagar to go back to Sarai and submit to her authority.

It's incredible to think that the almighty Lord God, who was trying also to work with Abram and Sarai and teach them lessons of faith, would see the misery in the heart of an "outsider"—Hagar—enough so that He visited her by a spring in the desert. Hagar named the spring Beer-lahairoi, which means "Well of the Living One who sees me." That is the antidote to loneliness—to be seen, to be visible—especially to God!

LONELINESS CAUSED BY REJECTION

> You have put away my acquaintances far from me;
> You have made me an abomination to them.
>
> —Psalm 88:8

Hagar's son, Ishmael—meaning "God hears"—grew. You know the rest of the story: A miracle happened and Sarah and Abraham became parents in their old age to the child of promise, Isaac. At a big celebration for Isaac (he was probably about three, and Ishmael was probably an early teen), Sarah saw Ishmael teasing Isaac. Having had sons, it's completely believable to me that an early teen would tease a little boy. But Sarah was incensed and told Abraham that Hagar and Ishmael had to go: "Get them out of here!"

We see a sad picture of Abraham, who had to be feeling the loss of his oldest son, putting together a care package and some water for Hagar and Ishmael as the "outsiders" left. As they wandered alone in the desert their water soon ran out, and Hagar became convinced they were going to die out there. She put Ishmael under the shade of a bush, walked away about a hundred yards, and wept. "I don't want to watch the boy die," she said (Gen. 21:16 NLT).

Again, God visited Hagar in her loneliness and opened her eyes to see a well of water, which revived them and helped them get on their way. Scripture says that God was with them as the boy grew and became an expert archer; and his mother arranged a marriage for him with a young woman from Egypt.

In this story of Hagar, we see that sometimes people get caught in isolated and awkward situations through no fault of their own. It was not Hagar's fault that she was in that desperate, no-win situation. If you are in such a place, remember that "God sees us" and that it is not His will that we be stuck in destructive places. And although we can't always choose what happens to us, we can choose our response—even in the midst of a lonely situation.

Life is full of injustice. If we look, it's all around us. *Why?* we wonder. It doesn't make sense, and at times, human suffering is almost too much to take in. We teach and believe that what we sow, we reap. And for much of life, that is true. Yet there are times of injustice. My daughter has struggled all her life by being "different"—she's Asian in a mostly Caucasian world. She's my daughter as much as any mother can have a daughter; yet she's constantly reminded of her heritage by others' comments. Someone will ask, "Amy, who's your real mother?" Or we'll be together in a store and the clerk will ask, "Are you an exchange student?" We laugh and try to keep a sense of humor about it, but there are constant reminders to Amy that she's different. In spite of this, Amy's reminded that she can choose her response.

What is comforting about the story of Hagar is seeing that although she was a victim, eventually she got out on her own and built a life. It began, though, by her understanding that "God saw her" in her misery, in her dire straits, and that He would provide for her.

LONELINESS BECAUSE OF CIRCUMSTANCES

> How shall we sing the LORD's song in a foreign land?
> —Psalm 137:4

Do you ever think, *Why is my life like this . . . so lonely? It seems that everyone else is having a good time except me.* But the person doesn't exist who hasn't at one time or another suffered from loneliness. How desperately we do need one another, especially when we are in a desert experience. The solution to loneliness is to offer to others what we ourselves are needing and not wait for others to make the first move.

Often we have a sense of being lonely as we go through certain passages in life: adolescence, midlife, the later years. Gail Sheehy, in writing about the passages of life, notes: "The older we grow, the more we become aware of the commonality of our lives, as well as our essential aloneness as navigators through the human journey."[1]

But through the changes of life we must keep reaching out, or we can become very isolated and lonely. Samuel Johnson said in 1755, "If a man does not make new acquaintances as he advances through life, he will soon find himself left alone. A man, sir, should keep his friendships in constant repair." It was true in the eighteenth century and it certainly is true now.

Loneliness can come in the older years. It becomes harder

to get out; our friends pass away or become ill; we lose a spouse; we quit making new friends, and our circle gets smaller and smaller. We can sit in that loneliness, or we can give out of it.

How simple, yet how easily we can ease someone else's loneliness. A phone call. A note. Lunch with a friend. Taking the time to ask good questions. My husband's uncle Bob was gifted at asking good questions. I remember at family gatherings he would pose questions that would help draw people out, which led to thoughtful discussions that helped family members feel understood, heard, and seen.

FINDING WATER IN THE DESERT

Love remains the vocation of all who are baptized, and love is a sign of God to the whole community. Yet love hurts. Here it is that some of us make our most costly mistakes. Here it is often that our personal story looks most wobbly and incomplete. Here it is, also, that we come to know God not only as our Creator, but as our redeemer, our lover, the hound of heaven who will not let us go.

—ANGELA TILBY[2]

How wonderful to be with others who love us and understand us. To laugh! It is indeed water in a dry and thirsty land. The solution to loneliness is being visible to someone, being understood by someone—belonging. It's knowing you are loved and vital to someone else. Jesus says, "You can love, because I first loved you." And yet some of us find it hard to believe so we accept teaspoonfuls of His love, and are then able to give only teaspoonfuls of it away. Why are we often afraid to love and be loved, afraid to reach out to others? Maybe it's a fear that we'll be taken advantage of or that our worth isn't quite up to complete acceptance by others.

We all long to be understood, but to be understood, we must risk facing—and telling—the truth. Some time ago, two friends and I were having tea, and one of my friends said, "I feel for you, Nancie, because some people put you on a pedestal. That must be hard."

That was my opening, and I took a deep breath. "Well, frankly, I'm not doing well. My pride keeps me insisting, 'I can handle this,' but I can't." Then I broke down and cried as my friends put their arms around me and prayed for me. Their arms, their prayers, said enough. When they left, my burden was lighter. My laughter was real and my smile genuine. What a wonderful thing it is to be loved, warts and all.

I received healing as I confessed to my friends that I didn't have it all together. James 5:16 says, "Confess your [faults] to one another, and pray for one another, that you may be healed." Our transient, busy lives can contribute to loneliness. It's hard to take time for relationships with so many other things that we must do.

REACHING OUT DISPELS LONELINESS

A friend is a gift you give yourself.

—ROBERT LOUIS STEVENSON

Often we protest being in a desert experience: "I don't want this reversal, I don't want this loss, I don't want this illness, this interruption."

And yet finally when we get there, we can grow accustomed to it. Like Hagar, we make a home there. We get used to being a victim, a martyr. We grow comfortable with our identity as a loner, and then we don't risk reaching out. But reaching out will dispel the loneliness. Certain beliefs keep us from opening up:

- Other people don't struggle with the kinds of problems I have.
- He or she can't possibly be my friend, based on position, wealth, appearance, and so on. What do I have to offer?
- If I let you get close to me, you won't like the real me. I'm afraid of being rejected or thought stupid, inferior, or whatever. This is my identity; I am a loser; I am an "outsider." I'm going to believe what people say about me.
- I was vulnerable once, and I was hurt, so never again. I'll put up my walls because it's too risky.

Richard Foster wrote, in *Celebration of Discipline,* "The discipline of confession brings an end to pretense. God is calling into being a church that can openly confess its frail humanity and know the forgiving and empowering graces of Christ. Honesty leads to confession, and confession leads to change."[3]

The greatest thing," says someone, "a man can do for his Heavenly Father is to be kind to some of His other children." I wonder why it is that we are not all kinder than we are? How much the world needs it! How easily it is done! How instantaneously it acts! How infallibly it is remembered! How superabundantly it pays itself back — for there is no debtor in the world so honorable, so superbly honorable, as love. "Love never faileth" . . . You will find as you look back upon your life that the moments that stand out, the moments when you have really lived, are the moments when you have done things in a spirit of love . . . Everything else in all our lives is transitory.

— HENRY DRUMMOND, *The Greatest Thing in the World*[4]

THE POWER OF A FRIEND

Friendship is the comfort, the inexpressible comfort of feeling safe with a person, having neither to weigh thoughts nor measure words, but pouring all right out just as they are, chaff and grain together, certain that a faithful hand will take and sift them, keep what is worth keeping, and with a breath of comfort, blow the rest away.

—GEORGE ELIOT[5]

———————————————◄◊►———————————————

When our son Eric was three, he had an imaginary friend he named Charlie Beakey. Eric was the middle child then, with Jon a couple of years older, and Chris the baby. At the time, Bill and I were busy working in the church with youth and music. To add to our hectic schedule, we moved to a new area, leaving behind all that was familiar to Eric. Charlie Beakey became Eric's best friend. Charlie never argued; he played whatever game Eric wanted to play; and he was always there when he needed him. After a year or two, though, Eric replaced Charlie Beakey with real friends.

Someone sent me a card with the inscription, "A friend is the relationship you need to help you through your other relationships." My friends help define life to me, and I need them. I know there have been times when I haven't been there as I should have for my friends. I have been known to be so late with birthday cards that the recipient thinks I am early. But my friends are forgiving and faithful, and I am humbly grateful. To have a friend, we must be one.

Although none of us are perfect, there is one perfect Friend—available to all of us. The very same One who saw

Hagar, the outsider, crying in the desert. John 13 through 17 describes Jesus and His disciples during the Passover in the Upper Room just before Jesus was crucified. Jesus had poured His life into these men, eating and sleeping and being with them for three years. "You are My friends," He said as He washed their feet, prayed for them, and broke bread with them. Jesus then gave some of His most eloquent and profound teachings, sharing insights and treasures from the Father with these, His dearest friends. In the group, of course, was Judas, who betrayed the Lord for thirty pieces of silver. We expect bad things from Judas—but the rest of the disciples, how could they have been so unfaithful? In the Garden of Gethsemane, Jesus asked: "Could you not watch one hour?" (Mark 14:37). In His greatest agony, they weren't there for Him.

I can understand the disciples being afraid. They didn't want to get the same treatment Jesus got, and it certainly seemed possible, with the ugly mood of the crowd and the Roman officers. How was it, though, that these men who'd followed Him night and day and pledged undying loyalty could go from discussing lofty thoughts of the eternal only to fall apart when He needed them the most and leave Him alone? To not even be able to stay awake and pray?

I'd like to think I would have been there for Jesus. I wouldn't have panicked. I wouldn't have been petty; I would have prayed with Him in His great agony, even if I didn't understand what was going on. But I'm afraid I'm not that different from the disciples. I can look out for myself often at the expense of others, forgetting that Jesus told us that in order to truly love Him, we must love others—especially those who are lonely. Lonely people often can't offer us anything—they tend to be in powerless places; they may be "outsiders," invisible people.

Calvin Miller writes of how we need to be set free from the "slavery of our own centrality. For make no mistake, it is usually our centrality in our own lives that is the reason for our dark times. Christians are not called to be spotlight people . . . God disappears when we insist on the spotlight. Then we are truly alone . . . None are sent away empty from Christ except those who come to Him full of themselves."[6]

But Jesus never fails us and tenderly reminds us to love Him by loving others, to really see, really hear people. When my brothers and sisters and I were little, sometimes our mother would hug us, look in our faces, and ask, "What does it feel like to be you?" We felt so loved by our mother because we were visible to her, each of us in our individuality.

Hagar must have had some bonding, some love for Abraham as the father of her son. And yet as he forced her to leave, he was telling her that he didn't want to "see" her or her son, Ishmael, ever again. I can only imagine the deep rejection she must have felt, the terror of being isolated in the desert. But then how wonderful to think of the comfort and delight of having God Himself speak to her in that place as He let her know that *He saw her; He understood her; He would be with her.* And most of all, He loved her. She was not alone after all.

— REFLECTION —

Think of an instance in your life when you were in a lonely or isolated place.

How did you respond? If you could, would you change the way you responded? What is hard about being lonely? Is there anything good about it? How can it help you relate to others?

— PRAYER —

Lord, I ask for an understanding of Your love. I have seen distorted love, and I need the healing power of Your gracious care for me. Thank You for giving me the gift of free will—that I can choose my response when I feel overwhelmed by loneliness. Give me courage to walk step-by-step in new places of freedom and confidence as I take risks to reach out to others who may be lonely. In Jesus' name. Amen.

~

Pray remember what I have recommended to you, which is, to think often on God, by day, by night, in your business, and even in your diversions. He is always near you and with you; leave Him not alone. You would think it rude to leave a friend alone who came to visit you; why, then, must God be neglected? Do not, then, forget Him, but think on Him often, adore Him continually, live and die with Him; this is the glorious employment of a Christian. In a word, this is our profession; if we do not know it, we must learn it.

—BROTHER LAWRENCE,
The Practice of the Presence of God (c. 1666)[7]

9

◌

THE DESERT OF WAITING

I waited patiently for the LORD;
    he turned to me and heard my cry.
He lifted me out of the slimy pit,
    out of the mud and mire;
he set my feet on a rock
    and gave me a firm place to stand.
He put a new song in my mouth,
    a hymn of praise to our God.
Many will see and fear
    and put their trust in the LORD.
                        —Psalm 40:1–3 NIV

— SUGGESTED READING: ACTS 1:1–14;
GENESIS 12–14, 16–18; 21:1–7; PSALM 37 —

WHAT GOOD IS WAITING?

Rest in the LORD, and wait patiently for Him.
                        —Psalm 37:7

O ne fall day I took a walk to a hidden lake not far from
our home. The sky was deep blue, the lake rimmed
by aspen trees turning yellow. The reflection of the trees on

the lake was so clear it was almost like a double picture. *Be like this*, it seemed God was saying. *When you are still before Me, you can then reflect Me.*

Yes, I want that, I thought, but I couldn't help wondering, *What's wrong with a creek running through the meadow? It gets more places, sees more things.* I do like to go places.

It's hard for me to be still, to wait. Waiting doesn't feel productive; it feels like wasted time. Earlier, I had sat at my kitchen table, savoring a cup of freshly brewed French roast as I evaluated my "to do" list and next year's calendar. I'd emitted a deep sigh as I realized again how crammed full life was, no matter how hard I tried to eliminate things. Life just kept coming with the kids' schedules, Bill's schedule, my schedule, our schedule, church activities, magazine deadlines. And I had just tried to cram more in by registering for a class at the local community college. I crossed out the class times with my pencil, realizing there was no way I could fit them in. I wondered, *How can I "be still and know God" in such a hectic world, and however do I "wait on God" when I'm always in a hurry?* My life didn't seem to be compatible with waiting.

Silence is the very presence of God — always there. But activity hides it. We need to leave activity long enough to discover the Presence—then we can return to activity.

—BASIL PENNINGTON[1]

LEARNING FROM MARY (ACTS 1)

Mary quietly treasured these things in her heart and
thought about them often.

—Luke 2:19 NLT

Mary, the mother of Jesus, is a wonderful example of
what it means to wait on God. Much of her life was spent
waiting. She spent time with her cousin Elizabeth, waiting
for Jesus to be born. After Jesus was born, she waited as
she watched Him grow, wondering what her amazing son
would do and become. After His ministry began, she waited
as she watched His ministry develop. At the Crucifixion,
she waited at the foot of the cross. She waited at the tomb.
And after Jesus ascended to heaven, she waited in the
upper room with the rest of the believers—fifty days—for
the promised gift of the Holy Spirit.

How tremendous it must have been for Mary to see the
Holy Spirit poured out at Pentecost and to be in the midst
of the excitement as the church began with many believing in her son Jesus. All those earlier years of wondering
and waiting now came into focus. Her waiting had not
been idleness; it was an active waiting. As she waited, she
did what needed to be done—took care of family needs,
went to weddings! She was submissive to God in her spirit
and she trusted, even though the whole picture was not
yet clear. No doubt her thoughts went back often to the
angel's words . . . the shepherds' visit . . . the wise men's
gifts, and she trusted for the future as she waited.

LEARNING FROM SARAH AND ABRAHAM
(GENESIS 12–14; 16–18; 21:1–7)

Hundreds of years before, God had called Abraham and Sarah out of their land and promised that Abraham would be the father of a great nation, that all the families of the earth would be blessed through him. They began their journey to believe God, but twenty-five years went by and still they had no children. Since they were getting on in years, Sarah suggested Abraham have a child by her handmaiden, Hagar. Sarah didn't wait for God's timing; instead she devised her own plan to help God along, which ultimately created all kinds of problems.

Finally, God gave Sarah and Abraham a son—Isaac, meaning "laughter." I read the passages in Genesis, trying to get a picture of how Sarah and Abraham waited. They did a lot of journeying, going from place to place. They took a side road to Egypt, where Abraham had to learn some important lessons about truth-telling. While he waited, he also took care of business at hand—his livestock; he mentored his nephew Lot, helped him get established. When Lot was kidnapped, Abraham took an army to rescue him. Abraham also interceded for people in the cities of Sodom and Gomorrah before their destruction.

So their waiting, too, was an *active waiting*. They dealt with life's responsibilities while they waited for God's timing. Yes, they made mistakes—Abraham's dishonesty; Sarah's manipulation—and they suffered consequences.

But they learned by their mistakes, and they are listed in Hebrews' great "Hall of Faith" (11:8–19).

We, too, can wait with an "active" waiting. I tried to learn this as I began to put aside many of my activities that (although good) were distracting and tried to focus on the "business at hand"—first of all, my husband and my children, then my writing and speaking, and while doing this, making my walk with God a priority. As I look back over the last ten years of my attempts to truly wait on God, I have much to learn. But I am finding that waiting on God in our fast-paced world is absolutely essential—and possible.

Andrew Murray writes about waiting on God:

> Before you pray, bow quietly before God, and seek to remember and realize who He is, how near He is, how certainly He can and will help. Just be still before Him, and allow His Holy Spirit to waken and stir up in your soul the child-like disposition of absolute dependence and confident expectation. Wait upon God as a Living Being, as the Living God, who notices you, and is just longing to fill you with His salvation. Wait on God till you know you have met Him; prayer will then become so different . . . let there be intervals of silence, reverent stillness of soul, in which you yield yourself to God, in case He may have aught He wishes to teach you or to work in you. Waiting on Him will become the most blessed part of prayer, and

161

the blessing thus obtained will be doubly precious as
the fruit of such fellowship with the Holy One.[2]

WAITING HELPS YOU NOTICE

My eyes are ever on the LORD.

—Psalm 25:15 NIV

Waiting improves your vision, your hearing, your senses.
You become aware of this if you ever have to wait an hour
or two in an airport or at a shopping mall. But until you sit
down and watch, you don't really notice what's going on
around you. Before, you're primarily focused on your own
activity and agenda. But when you stop and wait, you
become aware of other people, other conversations.

I was a skinny ten-year-old with a tangled mass of blonde
hair who loved being outside my Montana home every
spare minute, no matter the season. I was a true tomboy,
climbing trees, playing in the barn. I loved the winter when
the air was so cold it hurt to breathe and the snow sparkled
like diamonds so that you had to shield your eyes to look. I
loved the springtime and the meadowlarks that would sing
mornings and evenings on the fence behind our house. I
loved the summer when the lilacs in our front yard would
bloom and the rolling thunderstorms would sweep across
the sky to pour rain—and sometimes hail—upon the parched
earth. That's when I would run lickety-split into the house
with my brothers and sisters before the crashing lightning

came too close and we'd stand at the screen door, mesmer-ized. I loved the subtle cooling of the earth that said winter was coming, even though it was still sunny in a watery sort of way.

The late autumn landscape in Montana is colored in shades of brown and gray and pale yellow. The leaves have fallen; the wheat has long been cut and the earth is going into a quiet phase. It is not a pretty time of year as there usually isn't even snow on the ground. It is from one of those autumn days that I have a cherished memory. Usually my mother was busy with housework or with some of the younger children, but for some reason this particular after-noon, she said to me, "Let's go for a walk," and just she and I took off across the fields. But the walk soon slowed to an amble as we began looking for dried leaves to make an arrangement. I will never forget the transformation: When we began our walk, it was across what I perceived as a dry, flat, boring landscape. Nothing. But as we stopped and took a second look, suddenly it seemed as if beauty began exploding everywhere. I had never seen such beauty . . . in dried weeds! Mother and I talked and laughed as we gath-ered weeds, exclaiming over some with exotic shapes. We'd see another clump in a ditch and we'd go after it, adding it to our armload.

I believe this vivid memory is significant because it speaks to my tendency to want to rush toward a goal, when often real progress comes when I do just the opposite: Stop. Wait. Look. What—or who—is right in front of me? Of course, it is God; it is my children, my husband, my friends. Precious people. Sometimes the nuances are subtle, and it takes being still to be aware of the beauty that God is presenting. The beauty is just being with Him, even in the arid places, and He says, "Take time to look a little closer . . . there's something beautiful here." The memory of that extraordinary afternoon with my mother is special because that walk across dry and dusty fields was transformed as we saw beauty in what only moments before had been a wasteland. It was such a delightful surprise.

And so is waiting on God. Waiting can seem like a desert. Yet when we take the time to be still—to be there—to see it, we become aware of the beauty. We can be so goal-oriented we miss the process. But in waiting, we try to match our steps to His; we stop and look and listen where He is looking and listening, and that's when we see. We wonder; we laugh and sing. "Truly my soul silently waits for God . . . He leads me beside still waters, He restores my soul . . . In returning and rest shall be my confidence."

I began to realize that I wanted to wait on God; to really see what was in front of me. But I had to cultivate waiting; to give it time and to learn to read Scripture with an open mind and open heart, reflecting on what I read, and then trying to live what God's Word said. Waiting on God is an inner waiting to listen for His still, small voice. Sometimes waiting does mean to stop, to pause. But waiting on God isn't an empty waiting; it's a pregnant waiting, a waiting for the Holy Spirit to birth something wonderful as we watch for what He will do, knowing that He does all things well.

God does not cease speaking, but the noise of the creatures without, and of our passions within, deafens us, and stops our hearing. We must silence every creature, we must silence ourselves, to hear in the deep hush of the whole soul, the ineffable voice of the spouse. We must bend the ear, because it is a gentle and delicate voice, only heard by those who no longer hear anything else.

—FÉNELON[3]

WAITING TEACHES TRUST

My soul, wait silently for God alone,
For my expectation is from Him.
He only is my rock and my salvation;
He is my defense;
I shall not be moved.

—Psalm 62:5–6

It seems that I never stop waiting—there's always something to wait for. Now my husband and I are waiting for our house to sell. After much trepidation and trauma, we put the "For Sale" sign up in front of our house and lots of people have come through—with no offers. Month after month, we wait. We are tempted to ask, "Why, Lord? We're trying to do the right thing. How long is this going to take?" But maybe we're not at the place of brokenness yet, where we can give more freely of ourselves for God's purposes. Regardless, it's a good place to exercise trust and obedience. So for whatever the purpose is, we are determined to wait.

Psalm 37 tells us what to do while we wait, and the consequences of waiting:

ACTION	CONSEQUENCE
Trust in the Lord.	He will give the desires of your heart.
Feed on His faithfulness.	He will bring forth your righteousness as the light and your justice as noonday.
Commit your way to Him.	He will bring it to pass.
Rest in the Lord, wait patiently.	Your steps will be ordered by the Lord.
Do not fret because of evildoers.	You will inherit the earth.

When we wait, our eyes are on the Lord. Not on our problem, not on our need—but on the Lord. Waiting means to let Him have the things that hold us. And when we wait for Him, we don't wait alone; He is there, even though He may be silent.

"Waiting" does not mean to be in control, but to wait for the Holy Spirit's empowerment and leading. And while waiting is a time to look for the future, it's also a time to look back. Here is the truth I have seen in looking back: God has never failed us in the past; He won't fail us now. So as I look back, I can believe for today, believe for the future.

Trust Him. Learn what it means to hide your soul in Him in this way, in utter trust. After that, your prayers will be filled with true reverence—that is, a joyful respect not mixed with resentment, demands, or bargaining. For then our natural will is to have God himself—nothing less. And God's good will is simply to have us. To wrap us in himself, and in eternal life . . . This is the sturdy foundation on which everything else in your spiritual life depends, now and forever.

—JULIAN OF NORWICH, *I Promise You a Crown,*
PARAPHRASED BY DAVID HAZARD[4]

WAITING FOR THE RIGHT TIME

> He has made everything beautiful in its time. Also He
> has put eternity in their hearts, except that no one can
> find out the work that God does from beginning to
> end . . . I know that whatever God does, it shall be for-
> ever. Nothing can be added to it, and nothing taken
> from it.
>
> —Ecclesiastes 3:11, 14

Waiting on God is the most efficient use of time there is because we get in tune with Him. Waiting helps us adjust our senses, our inner hearing, our hearts, to His purposes, to align our spirits with His. Sometimes in the "waiting times," the winters of our souls, we may feel forgotten, that He is not there. But scripture tells us: "Surely [a nursing mother] may forget [her child], yet I will not forget you. See, I have inscribed you on the palms of My hands." The Amplified Version reads, "I have indelibly imprinted (tattooed a picture of) you on the palm of each of My hands" (Isa. 49:15–16).

Waiting can be a place of not knowing, a most difficult place, a place parents understand well. That's when the jury is still out, the story unfinished. As a parent, I want results now—to know everything is turning out right with my children! But Emerson wrote, "All I have seen teaches me to trust the Creator for all I have not seen." Trusting Him not knowing is an opportunity for my roots to go down deep, down where the nourishment is, to His Word, which is faithful and true. What is His message in uncertainty?

Simply that we must not cast away our confidence. There's a very still, small voice that says, *Trust Me. Put aside your striving and manipulating, and simply trust Me.* The prophet Isaiah declared,

> Have you not known?
> Have you not heard?
> The everlasting God, the LORD,
> The Creator of the ends of the earth,
> Neither faints nor is weary.
> His understanding is unsearchable.
> He gives power to the weak,
> And to those who have no might He increases strength.
> Even the youths shall faint and be weary,
> And the young men shall utterly fall,
> But those who wait on the LORD
> Shall renew their strength;
> They shall mount up with wings like eagles,
> They shall run and not be weary,
> They shall walk and not faint. (Isa. 40:28–31)

WAITING REFINES THE MESSAGE

The desert of waiting helps refine the message that God is writing on our lives.

It had been one of those weeks, full of interruptions and incessant demands. In the back of my mind was the weight of a spiritual retreat I was to lead beginning on Friday evening, and I was not ready. I had an outline of what I was to speak from, but I hadn't had quiet time to prepare my talks. Friday morning I had an idea: I would leave home early and stop by to see our son Andy. The retreat center was close to his college, and after we had lunch together, I would have at least two prime hours of quiet.

I picked Andy up at his apartment and moved over to let him drive. "You choose the place and I'll buy, Andy."

"Let's see . . ." He began to drive downtown. "There's a place I think you'd really like." *We're going downtown?* I thought. *Kind of out of our way. Today would be the day when he isn't in a hurry and I am!* Normally Andy was in a rush to get to a class or a basketball practice, and I would be doing well to grab a hug from him.

We found the restaurant and ordered, catching up on school and news from friends and relatives. Then Andy asked, "What are you going to speak about?" I started to answer flippantly, then I saw he really wanted to know, so I told him, "Well, tonight I'm going to talk about the gift of life that each of us has—how precious it is."

"That's cool. Say, Mom, isn't the cemetery close to here where Aunt Char and Uncle Bob's baby was buried?" He began asking questions about the little cousin he never knew; how her life was cut short at three months and how her death impacted the family. As we left the restaurant, Andy suggested, "Let's go visit the cemetery." It was a beautiful spring day and the vibrant colors of the flowering trees and rhododendrons and azaleas that are so plentiful in the Willamette Valley welcomed us.

We turned off a busy street onto a quiet side road and found the cemetery. It had been many years since I had been there and we walked back and forth, peering at stones, looking for the little name that was part of our extended family. I was about to give up when Andy called from a distance, "Here it is!" We brushed the newly cut grass off the stone and placed a flower on it. I swallowed hard, remembering the tears and unanswered questions. We were quiet for a moment, and then talked about life; how fragile it is, how often we take it all for granted. We slowly walked back to the car, and Andy commented how Aunt Char and Uncle Bob went on with life, pastoring, raising their other two daughters, going on to do missions work. "Nobody could understand why it happened, and it was hard, but they didn't get bitter," I replied. "They only became more committed, more compassionate. It reminds me of that quote, 'Only one life, 'twill soon be past; only what's done for Christ will last.'"

Later, as I waved to my lanky 6'3" son with his contagious smile, I suddenly thought how wonderful he was, and how grateful I was for him—for his life. How good it was to spend a sunny afternoon with him, and how rare. I drove to the retreat center, aware that somehow that afternoon I had been waiting on God, after all.

Waiting on God is not divorced from interruptions— from the side roads of life that teach us so eloquently, whether it is a shattering tragedy or a minor inconvenience. He speaks to us where we are, refining the message as we turn our ear to Him in the midst of it. I used to believe that to speak, to write books, I needed to generate knowledge from other places. While I have much to learn from reading and listening to others, I've learned that the most authentic material I have to deal with is me, and what it means to wait on God in my at-times messy, unpredictable life.

SEASONS OF LIFE

And now how do I wait? The waiting never stops, because as long as we live, seasons continue. Late this afternoon I walked in the cold stillness and the air had taken on an alpenglow, the sky nearly blending into the snow in a pale pink.

Winter is leaving, reluctantly. It doesn't leave easily here in the mountains, even though the red-winged blackbirds are back. And although I'm not sorry to see winter go, I do see the value of winter. It is a quiet time, a season to wait.

Each season is a precursor of the next. Without winter, there would be no spring with its new life . . . no summer in full bloom . . . no fall with its harvest. Winter is the time when we ponder what's gone on before. We think about future plantings, what we may do differently. But for this moment, the fields lie fallow as the seed dies, is buried, covered by snow, pelted by rain. And then it seems we wait forever for warmth, for sun again, for new growth, for the thaw. For things to move. And now that joyous time is coming when we will see tiny buds on trees and the crocuses will begin to poke their little green leaves out of the ground. The waiting will be over, for now.

So it is with the waiting times of our lives. But we can wait with confidence because we know that He is at work, even in the long, silent waiting. He is in today as well as tomorrow, and it's up to us to stay close to Him, trusting that He is working all things to our good.

And now, all glory to God, who is able to keep you from stumbling, and who will bring you into his glorious presence innocent of sin and with great joy. All glory to him, who alone is God our Savior, through Jesus Christ our Lord. Yes, glory, majesty, power, and authority belong to him, in the beginning, now, and forevermore. Amen.

—Jude 24–25 nlt

— Reflection —

In your waiting, memorize a scripture that speaks to you, and "pray it back" to God. Then be silent in His presence. Wait on Him; prayerfully open up your heart, your spirit to Him. Take a moment to reflect on your life this last year. What are you learning about waiting on God?

— PRAYER —

Lord, You said that if we wait upon You, You will renew our strength. That is exactly what I need, but it seems to go against my natural grain. I want to see results—now—and yet what good are "results" if they are not from You? Thank You for reminding me of where my true strength lies . . . and to wait upon You for Your timing, Your way, Your purpose. I submit my life, my time, everything to You, knowing You are in control. Lord, thank You for reminding me that You can bear the unbearable. May I truly know what it means that my burden is light because I am in Your loving hands. My eyes are ever on You, Lord, and in You I trust. Amen.

10

~

SURRENDER AND TRIUMPH IN THE DESERT

"But then I will win her back once again. I will lead
her out in the desert and speak tenderly to her there . . .
In that coming day," says the LORD, "you will call me
'my husband' instead of 'my master' . . . In that day,"
says the LORD, "I will answer the pleading of the sky
for clouds, which will pour down water on the earth
in answer to its cries for rain."

—Hosea 2:14, 16, 21 NLT

— SUGGESTED READING: THE BOOK OF HOSEA —

TRIUMPH COMES AFTER SURRENDER

A visit to the desert is a letting go of all things that
occupy one; therefore the desert represents a "nothing" or a nothingness experience. One is refreshed
in this desert.

—MATTHEW FOX[1]

Like Hosea's unfaithful wife, we are often drawn into
the desert so that God may speak tenderly to us
there, to draw us close to Him. Your life and my life are

developing stories that we are writing with God, and when we surrender to Him, we become a willing participant in our story. It can be hard for us to surrender at times, to allow Him to love us; we are proud, independent. But when we finally reach the place of letting go of trying to solve our own human dilemmas, He is there in an instant, carrying us through with the grace and love we so desperately need.

Surrender—the "letting go and letting God"—is a prerequisite to triumph. Triumph is an individual victory. I believe it is overcoming the adversity that is unique to that one. One's life may parallel another's, with obvious similarities—yet one person will triumph and another will be defeated, depending on his or her response to the adversity. Each life is truly a complex miracle with its own set of difficulties, gifts, and challenges. The people who really intrigue me are old, perhaps because they are stories nearly completed, and I love to listen to them talk, to hear their views of life. Much went into them to make them that way, and some stories are triumphant, some not.

THE STRUGGLES OF ANCESTORS

In my antique hutch I have some brown-toned pictures of my parents, my grandparents, and other ancestors. Their soft and expressionless faces grace my buffet. As I dusted the leather frames, I wondered, *What did they know of struggle? Of stress and depression and loss and guilt?* The serene pictures never seemed to be anything more to me than decorative pieces. Until recently, that is.

Last year I was asked to speak in Regina, Saskatchewan, and as I began to make travel plans I realized it was near to both my mother's and father's families of origin. Mother had wistfully said several times how much she'd like to go back there to visit. And we meant to take her—we just never got around to it before she died, as my siblings and I were in busy child-rearing years.

And Lignite, North Dakota, where my father was born, seemed to be on the way to nowhere—flat, dry farmland and bitter winters. No one would ever want to go there . . . but this opportunity was too close to pass up, so instead of making flight arrangements, I called my sisters and asked, "Are you in?" And thus began a memorable adventure.

I have never been much for tracing family history, although I treasure my parents and the only grandparent I ever knew, my mother's mother. But my father's parents died when he was very young, and my mother's father died in an institution in 1940, so none of these people seemed real to me. And yet as my three sisters and my sister-in-law and I began this meandering trip on back roads to retrace our family history, I began to be aware that this was a significant journey.

A Scavenger Hunt

We left Oregon, going through Montana where we all were raised and where our brother now farms. To retrace where our parents' lives began, we drove east across Montana and began what became a scavenger hunt of sorts as we poked about in small towns and cemeteries. Montana had always seemed big but now was enormous as we drove and drove. Our first stop was in Wolf Point, and we found the church where our mother went one night—very reluctantly—to hear her beloved older brother preach. That night our mother gave her life wholeheartedly to Jesus. Talk about desert! Like Hagar, she was an "outsider." She had had a child out of wedlock, a great shame then. She had been betrayed and rejected by someone she loved. Mother tried to make the best of her situation, though. She was famous for her red hair, her wonderful sense of humor with which she covered her pain. But as Mother's life took on new meaning, she never stopped being fun; instead her life deepened as her love for Scripture and Jesus infected everyone around her for the rest of her life.

My sisters and I drove around the little town that was so far out on the plains, isolated. Lonely. My oldest sister had vague memories of that time when she was just a little girl living with Mother and our grandmother, who cared for my sister as Mother worked as a hairdresser in the little town. As we drove, we tried to imagine the existence they had. How wonderful that Jesus found my mother in that desert of loneliness and came to her, giving her a love that would never let her go, never betray her . . . as He never did.

On we drove to Lignite, North Dakota, where years ago our father's father was pastor of the Bethany Swedish

Lutheran Church. They were good people, and he and his wife had six young children when he died at age thirty-nine of a ruptured appendix. Devastated, his widow remarried not long after and had three more young children. Tragically, the stepfather also died; then my father's mother died as well at age forty-three, leaving nine orphans, my father the second oldest son. Surely they must have felt like Job. *God, why would You allow this to happen? We've been righteous . . . we've tried to give to others, live a good life. Why so many losses?*

When my father was twenty-one, he began attending revival meetings in town, and one night, Jesus' call to him was irresistible. He realized being "good" wasn't enough— and the night he was saved his life radically changed. As we saw where my father's family lived, the still-tidy and proud town of our father's birth, we understood a little more about him. About us. My sisters and I found the neatly tended Bethany Cemetery in Lignite where our grandparents were buried and placed roses on their graves. Finally the grandchildren—now middle-aged—had come to visit.

A PAIN-FILLED STORY

On we drove across the border into Canada, looking for the birthplace of our mother in Tribune, Saskatchewan, and the grave of our grandfather. There was pain in this story as well. Our search bogged down and we finally enlisted the help of the local fire department, whose director graciously drove ahead of us because, as he said, "It's too hard to explain." We followed him back to where we had originally looked for the grave of our grandfather and realized why we hadn't found it.

Our grandfather had been a patient most of his life in a mental institution, and when he died, he was buried in a cemetery adjacent to the regular one. There were no markers for the mental patients. However, two of my cousins recently had gone to a great deal of trouble to find where he was buried and saw to it that a marker was placed on his grave. The desert of depression was a terrible place . . . and there had seemed to be no real help for our grandfather, no healing for his mental affliction—and although we had more questions than answers, it seemed he had died alone.

We stood at the new marker with our grandfather's name on it, all of us now suddenly in tears for this man we'd never met, never knew. Even in death he was still shamed; still an outsider. But now we had found his final resting place, and my sisters and I joined hands and thanked God for His faithfulness to us as a family . . . for being a Father to the fatherless—our mother—and leading her many hundreds of miles and years later to my father. Our father gave her the home and stability she'd never known; she gave him laughter and music that he'd never known. Their common bond as long as they lived was their burning passion for Jesus and their seven children. Jesus met both of our parents in their desert places of bitter loss and rejection and had quite literally taken them from the miry clay, set their feet on solid rock. And in the process, they'd been given a new song . . . a song of praise. The gentle and nourishing rain of Jesus changed their desert into a garden.

SISTERS

As my sisters and I drove to the conference where we participated and then drove the hundreds of miles back home, you can imagine we talked. And talked! How sisters do talk. But the talking changed to reflection; to what we'd seen, what we'd noticed. Tentatively at first, we shared our own desert experiences, telling each other things some of us had never shared before. Sisters should know everything about each other, and yet we can be proud, protective of our failures, of perhaps our silly worries.

We also talked about our joys . . . our children . . . our marriages. We laughed a lot, too. Yet as we talked there was something new, some release. A freedom from shame. I thought of my grandmother Olson's favorite hymn, "Marvelous Grace of Our Loving Lord," and my father's favorite, "Great Is Thy Faithfulness."

It seemed that this trip helped us understand in a fresh way that we don't have to put up fronts. As families and individuals, we all suffer desert experiences of failure and sin and loss. People always have. We all are tempted to be ashamed of some things; to feel we are "outsiders," that we must work hard at being good. But Jesus makes the difference as we come wholeheartedly to Him, knowing He cleanses us and calls us His own, loving us unconditionally. None of our struggles are new; they just have different faces. Our same struggles plagued our grandparents and parents; they plague our children. Yet every day He pours out His mercies again and again.

TRUST

What were we looking for? Maybe the same thing that Isaac looked for as he went back to dig out the wells of his father Abraham. He needed water—but the wells were dry, dirt having been thrown in by the enemy. And yet as he doggedly dug out the old wells he found the water. We drove home reminded that regardless of what dirt the enemy may try to throw in our lives, we know where to find the Living Water for the rest of our journey for ourselves, for our children. Our parents trusted Him in the most difficult places imaginable, and He met them there. We can trust Him now for our own lives and for our children and grandchildren—come what may—and He will be there.

WHAT CAN WE HOLD ON TO
IN A DESERT EXPERIENCE?

You are the same,
And Your years will have no end.
The children of Your servants will continue,
And their descendants will be established before You.

—PSALM 102:27, 28

We can hold on to the truth that we are being *held* by Him—even when it doesn't feel like it. God is continuing to develop in us His character and a higher purpose as we surrender to Him. I have found that real spiritual victory and breakthrough come when I take the time to hear what is really going on at the heart of my life—the anxiety, the frustration, the longing—and then to give it to Him, to let it go. Oswald Chambers wrote, "The only thing I can give to God is 'my right to myself.' If I will give God that, He will make a holy experiment out of me, and God's experiments always succeed."[2]

Shortly after my father died on a cold January day many years ago, Mother gave me a black-and-white snapshot of Dad holding me when I was two years old. I cherish that picture, as there is something infinitely precious about being held by one's father.

Dad, a righteous man, was *planted* in God:

> "Blessed is the man
> Who walks not in the counsel of the ungodly,
> Nor stands in the path of sinners,
> Nor sits in the seat of the scornful;
> But his delight is in the law of the LORD,
> And in His law he meditates day and night.
> He shall be like a tree
> Planted by the rivers of water,
> That brings forth its fruit in its season,
> Whose leaf also shall not wither;
> And whatever he does shall prosper." (Ps. 1:1–3)

Being rooted and planted in God is like being held by Him in all seasons—the dry times and the well-watered times. Regardless of the situation, I must put down my roots deep to the Living Water and cling to Him when I think I understand, and especially when I don't; only knowing that He holds me and all that I commit to Him.

> The wilderness and the wasteland shall be glad for them,
> And the desert shall rejoice and blossom as the rose;
> It shall blossom abundantly and rejoice,
> Even with joy and singing.
>
> —ISAIAH 35:1–2

THERE IS MUCH WE CAN BELIEVE, NO
MATTER WHAT IS HAPPENING IN OUR LIVES

We can believe that in a changing world, we can cling to an unchanging God. Jesus is the same yesterday, today, and forever. Life may hold difficult things for us—inevitably, I believe we all suffer some kind of disappointment or loss, and although there is an enemy who actively seeks to destroy, a stronger truth is that "greater is He that is in us than he that is in the world."

We can believe that His Word never changes. We can believe Him, because His Word is faithful and true. I am more convinced than ever that we need not be afraid of facing our most perplexing and desperate needs because when we cry out to Him from that place, He meets us and restores us by His life-giving Word.

We can believe that His plans still call for us to carry His message here on earth. How amazing that we have this treasure in our earthen vessels, that He trusts us and uses us, imperfect as we are, to carry His message of hope and redemption to those around us. The desert experience can teach us eloquent lessons of humility and compassion for others who are struggling.

We can believe that in every ending, there is also a beginning. There are times we must let go to grab on to what's ahead, and what may seem like an ending can signal the possibility for a new dream. It is God's very nature and character to redeem and restore all that we surrender to Him.

Remembering the Desert

He turns a wilderness into pools of water,

And dry land into watersprings.

There He makes the hungry dwell,

That they may establish a city for a dwelling place,

And sow fields and plant vineyards,

That they may yield a fruitful harvest.

—Psalm 107:35–37

Going back to retrace our family history helped me remember the faithfulness of God, that truly He is the Redeemer. It has been painful to write about my own desert experiences because I again sensed some of the emotions of that time. And it's important to say here that although I was reluctant to initially embrace the desert experience as many of us naturally are), after awhile I grew accustomed to it—to being "sick." In some ways it was a convenient way of getting out of some of my obligations—I wasn't feeling well, and people understood. It was a good excuse to stop working so hard.

But just as a desert has a beauty all its own, it can be tempting to begin to shape one's identity to one's pain. In many ways, it's safer not to try to leave the desert because there it's possible to hide behind painful experiences and emotions. To leave means to confront oneself: Confront the realities of an imperfect life, of imperfect relationships and situations. And the challenges of life never end. While it's important to learn from the desert, there is a time to choose to go on to productivity, health, and involvement in life—not forgetting the lessons of the desert, but not *staying* there.

The psalmist said, "Behold, You desire truth in the inward parts, and in the hidden part You will make me to know wisdom" (Ps. 51:6). The inward part—the real me that still struggles at times—is the part where if I have the courage to pay attention and ask God to enter, *there* is where I truly learn wisdom. That is surrender. Triumph comes as we put our hope and trust in His Word, waiting for Him to show us the way through the desert.

I am left with an awe of God's provision *no matter what,* and I am passionate to share with others that if we invite God into our most difficult places, He will be there. I have learned to say, "My hope is in You, Lord!"

My life is still very busy, and my list of things to do never seems to get completely checked off. The temptation to accept inward pressure never ends, and life offers a continuing challenge of prioritizing and trying to discern how to live. I'll probably always be a busy person, and yet my life is richer as I am learning what it means to wait on God.

I try to live in the moment and savor the simple things of life that are so profound. Late this afternoon I stopped to see a breathtaking view of the setting sun behind the clouds and snow-covered mountains. I breathed in the beauty and said "Thank You" to God. I never want to lose the wonder of the beauty of God's world.

I've learned to thank God for the people and situations He's placed in my life, knowing they are gifts from Him. I'm learning to be an honest person, less manipulative of my husband and children . . . to love them with no strings attached. I've learned to be kinder to myself, to be more protective from the crush of life. I'm learning to be more courageous and truthful in my expressions. I've also learned that the mind-body connection is powerful. My life was clearly out of balance and was getting a strong wake-up call from my body to pay attention. It is true that we are fearfully and wonderfully made and God speaks to us through our pain, physically or emotionally.

The desert experience also gave me a sense of humility and compassion. Now I have greater empathy for those who are struggling. In *The Wounded Healer*, Henri Nouwen asks this poignant question: "'Who can take away suffering without entering into it?' The great illusion of leadership is to think that others can be led out of the desert by someone who has never been there."[3]

I have learned to set my hope in God. I would have said all along that that was where my hope was, but in truth it was not. It was in what I could do. I have learned to say, "My hope is in You, Lord!"

And He will cause the rain to come down for you . . .
And the vats shall overflow with new wine and oil.
So I will restore to you the years that the swarming
locust has eaten . . .

You shall eat in plenty and be satisfied,
And praise the name of the Lord your God,
Who has dealt wondrously with you;
And My people shall never be put to shame."

—JOEL 2:23–26

— REFLECTION —

Is there a desert experience that you need to surrender?
Perhaps it's something you are trying to solve on your
own. Consider specific steps that will help you surrender . . . to let go so that you can grab on to the next wonderful adventure that God has for you.

— PRAYER —

Father, I want to know Thee, but my cowardly heart
fears to give up its toys. I cannot part with them without inward bleeding, and I do not try to hide from
Thee the terror of the parting. I come trembling, but
I do come. Please root from my heart all those things
which I have cherished so long and which have become
a very part of my living self, so that thou mayest enter
and dwell there without a rival. Then shalt Thou
make the place of Thy feet glorious. Then shall my
heart have no need of the sun to shine in it, for Thyself

will be the light of it, and there shall be no night there. In Jesus' name. Amen.

— A. W. TOZER, *The Pursuit of God* [4]

"Let not the wise man glory in his wisdom,
Let not the mighty man glory in his might,
Nor let the rich man glory in his riches;
But let him who glories glory in this,
That he understands and knows Me,
That I am the LORD, exercising lovingkindness,
   judgment, and righteousness in the earth.
For in these I delight," says the LORD.

—JEREMIAH 9:23–24

ACKNOWLEDGMENTS

Thank you, Victor Oliver, for encouraging me to write about the desert experience. It was not easy to re-live some of the most difficult days of my life; and yet I'm reminded by this process of writing about the desert experience that it is in the hard places where God often speaks the clearest. And thank you, Cindy Blades and Kristen Lucas, for your editing support, and my gratitude to the rest of the fine staff of Thomas Nelson for their investment in this project.

Thank you, too, my friends (you know who you are!), for being willing to share your desert experiences and how God has met you there. May all of us become life-long listeners and learners!

And thank you, my wonderful children: Jon and Brittni, and Willy and Kendsy; Eric; Christian; Andrew; and Amy. You are my greatest joy and will be forever in my heart.

And my deepest thank you to Bill, my life-long love. Together we have experienced deserts and oases; how blessed we are by sunshine and rain. How blessed we are by His presence in all places.

ABOUT THE AUTHOR

Nancie Charmichael met her husband, Bill, at Southern California College, and they married in 1966. In her early married years, Nancie worked side by side with her husband in pastoral ministry, and then in the writing and publishing realm. Nancie has been involved since 1979 in publishing magazines with her husband. She is a former editor of *Virtue* magazine, where for several years she wrote articles, Bible studies, and the "Deeper Life" column. Nancie and Bill have written several books together.

In May of 1999, Bill and Nancie were awarded honorary doctorates from Western Baptist College the same day their youngest son graduated. They are parents to five children and grandparents to two.

Nancie speaks at a variety of women's conferences and retreats throughout the United States and Canada and has been involved in sponsoring conferences for women in prison for seventeen years. About her speaking, she says, "My passion is simply to share out of my own life—as a wife, mother and friend—the fact that we can trust Him no matter what life throws at us. If I'm sure of anything, I know that He redeems and restores ALL that we place in His hands."

NOTES

INTRODUCTION
1. Nancie Carmichael, *Desperate for God: How He Meets Us When We Pray* (Wheaton, Il: Crossway, 1998).

CHAPTER ONE: WHAT AM I DOING HERE?
1. Howard Thurman, *The Growing Edge,* quoted in *Disciplines for the Inner Life,* by Bob Benson and Michael W. Benson (Nashville: Thomas Nelson, 1989), 72.

2. A. W. Tozer, *Signposts: A Collection of Sayings from A. W. Tozer,* comp. Harry Verploegh (Wheaton, IL: Victor, 1988), 150.

CHAPTER TWO: THE DESERT OF LOSS
1. Thomas Merton, *No Man Is an Island* (San Diego: Harcourt Brace Jovanovich, 1955), 87.

2. Flora Slosson Wuellner, "When Prayer Encounters Pain," in *Weavings Reader: Living with God in the World* (Nashville: Upper Room, 1993), 87.

3. Bob Phillips, *Phillips' Book of Great Thoughts and Funny Sayings* (Wheaton, IL: Tyndale, 1993), 62.

4. Os Guinness, *The Call* (Nashville: Word, 1999).

5. St. Francis of Sales, quoted in *The Treasure Chest* (San Francisco: HarperSanFrancisco, 1995), 120.

6. Catherine Marshall, *My Personal Prayer Diary*, comp. and written by Catherine Marshall and Leonard LeSourd (New York: Ballantine, 1979), devotional from May 3.

CHAPTER THREE: THE DESERT OF PAIN
1. Whellner, *Weavings Reader*, 88.

2. Craig Barnes, *Yearning: Living Between How It Is and How It Ought to Be* (Downers Grove, IL: InterVarsity Press, 1992).

CHAPTER FOUR: THE DESERT OF EXHAUSTION
1. Thomas à Kempis, quoted in *The Treasure Chest* (New York: HarperCollins, 1959), 118.

2. Walter Brueggemann, *Finally Comes the Poet* (Minneapolis: Augsburg, 1989), 109.

3. M. Scott Peck, *Abounding Grace* (Kansas City, MO: Ariel Books, 2000), 187.

4 Basil Pennington, *A Place Apart* (Garden City, NY: Doubleday, 1983).

5. Kenneth L. Holmes and David C. Duniway, eds., *Covered Wagon Women: Diaries and Letters from the Western Trails, 1852*, vol. 5 (Lincoln, NE: University of Nebraska Press/Bison Books, 1995), 65.

6. Susan G. Butruille, *Women's Voices from the Oregon Trail* (Boise: Tamarack Books, 1994), 115.

CHAPTER FIVE: THE DESERT OF CIRCUMSTANCES
1. Merlin R. Carothers, quoted in *Doubleday Christian Quotation Collection* (New York: Doubleday, 1998), 248.

2. Victor Frankl, *Man's Search for Meaning* (New York: Simon & Schuster, 1984).

3. John of the Cross, *You Set My Spirit Free*, para. David Hazard (Minneapolis: Bethany House, 1994), 132.

CHAPTER SIX: THE DESERT OF WANDERING
1. Paul Tournier, *A Place for You* (New York: Harper & Row, 1968), 136.

2. Butruille, *Women's Voices from the Oregon Trail*, 123.

3. Madame Guyon, *The Way Out: The Study of Exodus* (Auburn, ME: Christian Books, 1985), 62.

4. Catherine Marshall, *Something More* (Carmel, NY: Guideposts Association, 1974), 33.

5. Olive Wyon, *Into His Presence: Spiritual Disciplines for the Inner Life,* ed. Ian Bunting (Nashville: Thomas Nelson, 1993), 361.

6. *Doubleday Christian Quotation Collection,* 156.

7. Andrew Murray, *With Christ in the School of Prayer* (New Kensington, PA: Whitaker House, 1981), 171.

8. Quoted in *Oswald Chambers: The Best from All His Books* (Nashville: Oliver-Nelson, 1989), 1.

9. John Baille, quoted in *The Harper Collins Book of Prayers,* comp. Robert Vande Weyer (Edison, New Jersey: Castle, 1997), 48.

10. *Chambers,* 210.

CHAPTER SEVEN: THE DESERT OF DEPRESSION

1. *Mayo Clinic Family Healthbook* (New York: Morrow, 1990), 227.

2. Calvin Miller, *Walking with Saints: Through the Best and Worst Times of Our Lives* (Nashville: Thomas Nelson, 1995), 121.

3. Anne Lamott, *Traveling Mercies* (New York: Pantheon, 1999), 65.

4. Lewis B. Smedes, *Shame and Grace* (San Francisco: HarperSanFrancisco, 1993), 109.

5. Henri Nouwen, *Seeds of Hope: A Henri Nouwen Reader* (New York: Bantam, 1989), 203.

6. Quoted in *Disciplines for the Inner Life,* 73.

7. Frank Minirth, Paul Meier, and Stephen Arterburn, *The Complete Life Encyclopedia* (Nashville: Thomas Nelson, 1995), 215–16.

8. James Houston, *The Transforming Friendship* (Oxford: Lion Publishing, 1989), 243.

9. Dag Hammarskjold, *Markings,* (New York: Knopf, 1964), 58.

CHAPTER EIGHT: THE DESERT OF LONELINESS
1. Gail Sheehy, *Passages* (New York: Bantam, 1976), 28.

2. Angela Tilby, in the *Doubleday Christian Quotation Collection,* 332.

3. Richard J. Foster, *Celebration of Discipline* (San Francisco: HarperSanFrancisco, 1978), 157.

4. Henry Drummond, *The Greatest Thing in the World*, in *Inspiration Three: Three Famous Classics* (New Canaan, CT: Keats Publishing, 1973), 17.

5. George Eliot, *The Treasure Chest*, comp. Wallis and Culhane, 97.

6. Miller, *Walking with Saints*, 57.

7. Brother Lawrence, *The Practice of the Presence of God*, in *Inspiration Three*, 103.

CHAPTER NINE: THE DESERT OF WAITING
1 Basil Pennington, *Centered Living* (New York: Doubleday/Image Book, 1988), 149.

2 Adapted from *Waiting on God*, by Andrew Murray (London: Nisbet & Co., 1895).

3 Fénelon, *Christian Perfection* (Minneapolis: Dimension Books, 1975), 155–56.

4 Julian of Norwich, *I Promise You a Crown*, para. David Hazard (Minneapolis: Bethany House, 1995).

CHAPTER TEN: SURRENDER & TRIUMPH
IN THE DESERT

1 Matthew Fox, quoted in *Doubleday Christian Quotation Collection*, comp. Hannah Ward and Jennifer Wild (New York: Doubleday, 1997), 263.

2 *Oswald Chambers: The Best from All His Books* (Nashville, TN: Thomas Nelson, 1989), 97.

3. Henri J. M. Nouwen, *The Wounded Healer* (New York: Doubleday, 1979), 40.

4. A. W. Tozer, *The Pursuit of God* (Camp Hill, PA: Christian Publications, 1982), 30.